PMI-PgMP Exam Ex

Q&A with In-Depth Expla
SUJAN MUKHERJE

PMI-PgMP Exam Excellence : Q&A with In-Depth Explanations
FIRST EDITION. September 8th, 2023.
COPYRIGHT © 2023 SUJAN.

Written by SUJAN MUKHERJEE.

CONTENTS

(Multiple-choice questions with Detailed Explanations)

Introduction

Welcome to "PMI-PgMP Exam Excellence: Q&A with In-Depth Explanations." This book is your essential companion on the path to achieving Program Management Professional (PgMP) certification.

The PgMP certification, accredited by the Project Management Institute (PMI), stands as a globally recognized testament to your expertise and leadership in program management. Attaining this certification not only marks a significant career milestone but also showcases your ability to deliver strategic results through effective program management.

Preparation is paramount when pursuing PgMP certification. This book is meticulously designed to equip you with the knowledge, strategies, and confidence required to excel in the PgMP exam. It is more than just a collection of questions and answers; it is a comprehensive learning resource that guides you through the intricacies of program management and ensures you possess the skills necessary to tackle the exam with proficiency.

What to Expect:

Inside, you'll find a diverse range of practice questions aligned with the PgMP exam format and content. These questions are supplemented with in-depth explanations to enhance your comprehension of program management principles.

Moreover, our book offers valuable insights and exam strategies to navigate the PgMP exam effectively. It comprehensively covers program management domains, from governance to benefits realization, ensuring you are well-prepared for the challenges that the exam may present.

With "PMI-PgMP Exam Excellence: Q&A with In-Depth Explanations," you're embarking on a transformative journey toward PgMP certification and an elevated program management career.

PRACTICE TEST - 1

1. Question

: What is the primary difference between program management and project management?

A) Program management focuses on short-term goals, while project management focuses on long-term objectives.

B) Program management deals with a collection of related projects, while project management focuses on individual projects.

C) Program management only involves technical aspects, while project management encompasses both technical and administrative tasks.

D) Program management is primarily concerned with risk mitigation, while project management focuses on cost control.

Answer: B) Program management deals with a collection of related projects, while project management focuses on individual projects.

Explanation: Program management involves coordinating and managing a group of related projects and initiatives, ensuring they align with organizational objectives, while project management focuses on executing individual projects within the program.

2. Question: Which of the following is NOT a component of the Program Management Life Cycle (PgMLC)?

A) Initiating

B) Executing

C) Controlling

D) Closing

Answer: B) Executing

Explanation: The Program Management Life Cycle includes Initiating, Planning, Executing, Monitoring and Controlling, and Closing phases. Executing is part of project management.

3. Question: What is the primary purpose of a Program Charter?

A) To provide a detailed project plan

B) To define the roles and responsibilities of team members

C) To authorize the program and establish high-level objectives

D) To track and monitor program progress

Answer: C) To authorize the program and establish high-level objectives

Explanation: A Program Charter is a document that authorizes the program and defines its high-level objectives, scope, and stakeholders.

4. Question: During the program initiation phase, which document is created to outline the scope, objectives, and stakeholders of the program?

A) Program Charter

B) Program Plan

C) Program Budget

D) Program Schedule

Answer: A) Program Charter

Explanation: The Program Charter is created during program initiation to define the program's scope, objectives, and stakeholders.

5. Question: What is the primary goal of program governance?

A) To increase program costs

B) To minimize program risks

C) To ensure compliance with regulations

D) To provide strategic oversight and direction

Answer: D) To provide strategic oversight and direction

Explanation: Program governance aims to provide strategic oversight and direction to ensure that the program aligns with organizational objectives.

6. Question: Which program management process involves identifying, assessing, and addressing risks that may impact the program's success?

A) Program Closure

B) Program Integration Management

C) Program Risk Management

D) Program Stakeholder Engagement

Answer: C) Program Risk Management

Explanation: Program Risk Management is the process of identifying, assessing, and addressing risks that may affect the program's success.

7. Question: What is the primary purpose of a Program Benefits Management Plan?

A) To define the program's budget

B) To identify and track program risks

C) To outline how program benefits will be realized and measured

D) To allocate resources to program activities

Answer: C) To outline how program benefits will be realized and measured

Explanation: A Program Benefits Management Plan outlines how program benefits will be realized, measured, and tracked throughout the program's lifecycle.

8. Question: In program management, what does the term "interdependency" refer to?

A) The reliance of programs on external funding sources

B) The relationship between program managers and stakeholders

C) The connections and relationships between program components and projects

D) The integration of program objectives with organizational goals

Answer: C) The connections and relationships between program components and projects

Explanation: Interdependencies in program management refer to the connections and relationships between different program components and projects.

9. Question: What is the primary objective of program evaluation and review technique (PERT) in program management?

A) To estimate the duration of program activities

B) To identify critical program risks

C) To allocate resources to program tasks

D) To track program expenditures

Answer: A) To estimate the duration of program activities

Explanation: PERT is a technique used to estimate the duration of program activities and identify critical paths.

10. Question: During the program closure phase, which activity is typically performed?

A) Initiating new projects within the program

B) Transitioning program deliverables to operations or maintenance

C) Revising the program charter

D) Expanding the program's scope

Answer: B) Transitioning program deliverables to operations or maintenance

Explanation: During program closure, program deliverables are typically transitioned to operations or maintenance for ongoing support and maintenance.

11. Question: What is the primary role of the Program Management Office (PMO) in program management?

A) To oversee individual projects within the program

B) To provide administrative support to program managers

C) To ensure compliance with program policies and procedures

D) To support program managers and provide guidance and governance

Answer: D) To support program managers and provide guidance and governance

Explanation: The PMO plays a crucial role in providing support to program managers and ensuring effective governance of the program.

12. Question: In program management, what is the purpose of a Program Roadmap?

A) To schedule program meetings and reviews

B) To outline the strategic goals of the program

C) To track program budget expenditures

D) To visualize the program's timeline and key milestones

Answer: D) To visualize the program's timeline and key milestones

Explanation: A Program Roadmap is used to visually represent the program's timeline, major milestones, and key activities.

13. Question: Which program management approach focuses on delivering value incrementally and frequently, adapting to changing requirements?

A) Agile Program Management
B) Waterfall Program Management
C) Traditional Program Management
D) Lean Program Management

Answer: A) Agile Program Management

Explanation: Agile Program Management emphasizes delivering value incrementally, adapting to changing requirements, and frequently reviewing and adjusting program activities.

14. Question: In program management, what is a Program Stakeholder Register used for?

A) To track program risks
B) To document program benefits
C) To identify and assess program stakeholders
D) To schedule program activities

Answer: C) To identify and assess program stakeholders

Explanation: A Program Stakeholder Register is used to identify and assess program stakeholders, their interests, and their influence on the program.

15. Question: Which program management framework emphasizes the importance of optimizing the flow of value across the entire program?

A) PMBOK (Project Management Body of Knowledge)
B) PRINCE2 (Projects IN Controlled Environments)
C) SAFe (Scaled Agile Framework)
D) ITIL (Information Technology Infrastructure Library)

Answer: C) SAFe (Scaled Agile Framework)

Explanation: SAFe is a framework that focuses on optimizing the flow of value across the entire program and aligning it with business objectives.

16. Question: What is the purpose of a Program Benefits Realization Report?

A) To document program risks

B) To track program schedule performance

C) To assess the realization of program benefits against expected outcomes

D) To create a detailed program budget

Answer: C) To assess the realization of program benefits against expected outcomes

Explanation: A Program Benefits Realization Report is used to assess whether program benefits have been realized as expected.

17. Question: Which program management role is responsible for defining and maintaining the program's vision and goals?

A) Program Manager

B) Program Sponsor

C) Program Coordinator

D) Program Stakeholder

Answer: B) Program Sponsor

Explanation: The Program Sponsor is typically responsible for defining and maintaining the program's vision and goals.

18. Question: What is the primary focus of program integration management?

A) Managing program risks

B) Coordinating program stakeholders

C) Ensuring alignment with organizational strategy

D) Documenting program processes

Answer: B) Coordinating program stakeholders

Explanation: Program Integration Management focuses on coordinating program stakeholders, activities, and components to achieve program objectives.

19. Question: Which program management technique involves ranking program projects based on priority and available resources?

A) Program Evaluation and Review Technique (PERT)

B) Earned Value Management (EVM)

C) Program Prioritization

D) Critical Chain Method (CCM)

Answer: C) Program Prioritization

Explanation: Program Prioritization involves ranking program projects based on priority and resource availability to make informed decisions.

20. Question: What is the primary purpose of a Program Change Request?

A) To document program risks

B) To request additional funding for the program

C) To propose changes to the program scope, schedule, or budget

D) To communicate program achievements to stakeholders

Answer: C) To propose changes to the program scope, schedule, or budget

Explanation: A Program Change Request is used to propose changes to the program's scope, schedule, or budget and assess their impact on the program.

21. Question: In program management, what is the primary purpose of a Program Governance Board?

A) To execute program activities

B) To approve changes to the program scope

C) To lead program teams

D) To create program schedules

Answer: B) To approve changes to the program scope

Explanation: A Program Governance Board is responsible for approving changes to the program's scope, ensuring alignment with strategic objectives.

22. Question: Which program management approach is best suited for situations where requirements are well-defined, and there is little uncertainty?

A) Agile Program Management

B) Waterfall Program Management

C) Lean Program Management

D) Adaptive Program Management

Answer: B) Waterfall Program Management

Explanation: Waterfall Program Management is most suitable when requirements are well-defined and there is minimal uncertainty in the program.

23. Question: What does the term "Benefits Dependency Map" refer to in program management?

A) A diagram showing the relationships between program benefits and stakeholders

B) A schedule of program benefits realization activities

C) A map of the geographical distribution of program benefits

D) A timeline of program benefits payments

Answer: A) A diagram showing the relationships between program benefits and stakeholders

Explanation: A Benefits Dependency Map visually represents the relationships between program benefits and stakeholders.

24. Question: Which document outlines the program's approach to communication and stakeholder engagement?

A) Program Charter

B) Program Benefits Management Plan

C) Program Communication Plan

D) Program Risk Register

Answer: C) Program Communication Plan

Explanation: The Program Communication Plan outlines how communication and stakeholder engagement will be managed throughout the program.

25. Question: What is the primary goal of the program stakeholder analysis process?

A) To identify and prioritize program benefits

B) To establish program governance

C) To identify and understand program stakeholders' interests and influence

D) To allocate resources to program activities

Answer: C) To identify and understand program stakeholders' interests and influence

Explanation: Program stakeholder analysis aims to identify and understand the interests and influence of stakeholders.

26. Question: Which program management framework emphasizes a standardized approach to project and program management processes?

A) PRINCE2 (Projects IN Controlled Environments)

B) SAFe (Scaled Agile Framework)

C) PMBOK (Project Management Body of Knowledge)

D) Lean Program Management

Answer: A) PRINCE2 (Projects IN Controlled Environments)

Explanation: PRINCE2 is a framework that emphasizes a standardized approach to project and program management processes.

27. Question: What is the primary purpose of a Program Quality Management Plan?

A) To allocate resources to program activities

B) To outline how program quality will be managed and assured

C) To track program schedule performance

D) To assess program risks

Answer: B) To outline how program quality will be managed and assured

Explanation: A Program Quality Management Plan outlines how program quality will be managed and assured throughout the program.

28. Question: Which program management process involves defining, documenting, and managing program requirements?

A) Program Risk Management

B) Program Scope Management

C) Program Change Control

D) Program Benefits Realization

Answer: B) Program Scope Management

Explanation: Program Scope Management involves defining, documenting, and managing program requirements.

29. Question: What is the primary goal of program financial management?

A) To ensure program compliance with regulations

B) To allocate resources to program activities

C) To track program schedule performance

D) To manage program finances efficiently and effectively

Answer: D) To manage program finances efficiently and effectively

Explanation: Program financial management focuses on managing program finances efficiently and effectively to achieve program objectives.

30. Question: In program management, what does the term "strategic alignment" refer to?

A) The alignment of program benefits with stakeholder interests

B) The integration of program components

C) The alignment of program objectives with organizational goals

D) The prioritization of program risks

Answer: C) The alignment of program objectives with organizational goals

Explanation: Strategic alignment in program management refers to the alignment of program objectives with the strategic goals of the organization.

31. Question: Which program management role is responsible for ensuring that program activities adhere to established policies and procedures?

A) Program Manager

B) Program Sponsor

C) Program Governance Board

D) Program Coordinator

Answer: C) Program Governance Board

Explanation: The Program Governance Board is responsible for ensuring program activities adhere to established policies and procedures.

32. Question: In program management, what is the primary purpose of a Program Business Case?

A) To document program risks

B) To outline the program's high-level objectives and expected benefits

C) To track program schedule performance

D) To allocate resources to program activities

Answer: B) To outline the program's high-level objectives and expected benefits

Explanation: A Program Business Case outlines the program's high-level objectives and expected benefits to support decision-making.

33. Question: Which program management approach emphasizes eliminating waste and maximizing value while minimizing resources?

A) Agile Program Management

B) Traditional Program Management

C) Lean Program Management

D) Waterfall Program Management

Answer: C) Lean Program Management

Explanation: Lean Program Management focuses on eliminating waste and maximizing value while minimizing resources.

34. Question: What is the primary purpose of a Program Risk Register?
A) To allocate resources to program activities
B) To document program benefits
C) To identify and assess program risks
D) To track program schedule performance
Answer: C) To identify and assess program risks
Explanation: A Program Risk Register is used to identify and assess program risks that may impact program success.

35. Question: Which program management technique involves tracking the progress of program activities based on their planned vs. actual performance?
A) Program Evaluation and Review Technique (PERT)
B) Earned Value Management (EVM)
C) Critical Chain Method (CCM)
D) Program Prioritization
Answer: B) Earned Value Management (EVM)
Explanation: Earned Value Management (EVM) involves tracking the progress of program activities based on their planned vs. actual performance.

36. Question: In program management, what is the primary purpose of a Program Dependency Matrix?
A) To track program risks
B) To visualize program benefits
C) To identify and manage interdependencies between program components
D) To allocate resources to program activities
Answer: C) To identify and manage interdependencies between program components
Explanation: A Program Dependency Matrix is used to identify and manage interdependencies between program components and activities.

37. Question: What is the primary objective of program procurement management?

A) To allocate resources to program activities

B) To identify and assess program risks

C) To manage the acquisition of goods and services for the program

D) To track program schedule performance

Answer: C) To manage the acquisition of goods and services for the program

Explanation: Program procurement management focuses on managing the acquisition of goods and services needed for the program's success.

38. Question: Which program management framework emphasizes a holistic approach to managing business change?

A) MSP (Managing Successful Programmes)

B) PRINCE2 (Projects IN Controlled Environments)

C) SAFe (Scaled Agile Framework)

D) PMBOK (Project Management Body of Knowledge)

Answer: A) MSP (Managing Successful Programmes)

Explanation: MSP emphasizes a holistic approach to managing business change through programs.

39. Question: What is the primary goal of program stakeholder engagement?

A) To eliminate program risks

B) To ensure compliance with program policies

C) To actively involve stakeholders in program decisions and activities

D) To create a detailed program budget

Answer: C) To actively involve stakeholders in program decisions and activities

Explanation: Program stakeholder engagement aims to actively involve stakeholders in program decisions and activities to ensure their support and alignment.

40. Question: In program management, what does the term "Value Stream Mapping" refer to?

A) A visual representation of the program schedule

B) A technique for assessing program risks

C) A process for identifying and optimizing the flow of value in a program

D) A method for documenting program benefits

Answer: C) A process for identifying and optimizing the flow of value in a program

Explanation: Value Stream Mapping is a process used in program management to identify and optimize the flow of value across program activities and processes.

41. Question: What is the primary purpose of a Program Benefits Dependency Map?

A) To allocate resources to program activities

B) To visualize program benefits

C) To identify dependencies between program benefits

D) To track program schedule performance

Answer: C) To identify dependencies between program benefits

Explanation: A Benefits Dependency Map helps identify dependencies between program benefits, helping to understand how they relate to one another.

42. Question: Which program management role is responsible for ensuring that program deliverables meet quality standards?

A) Program Manager

B) Program Sponsor

C) Program Quality Assurance Manager

D) Program Coordinator

Answer: C) Program Quality Assurance Manager

Explanation: The Program Quality Assurance Manager is responsible for ensuring that program deliverables meet quality standards.

43. Question: In program management, what does the term "Program Governance Framework" refer to?

A) A document outlining program governance principles and policies

B) The hierarchy of program governance roles

C) The program's timeline and milestones

D) The program's budget allocation

Answer: A) A document outlining program governance principles and policies

Explanation: A Program Governance Framework is a document that outlines the principles and policies governing program governance.

44. Question: What is the primary purpose of a Program Risk Response Plan?

A) To document program risks

B) To outline the program's risk mitigation strategies

C) To allocate resources to program activities

D) To track program schedule performance

Answer: B) To outline the program's risk mitigation strategies

Explanation: A Program Risk Response Plan outlines the strategies and actions to mitigate identified program risks.

45. Question: Which program management technique involves identifying and analyzing the strengths, weaknesses, opportunities, and threats associated with a program?

A) SWOT Analysis

B) Earned Value Management (EVM)

C) Value Stream Mapping

D) Critical Chain Method (CCM)

Answer: A) SWOT Analysis

Explanation: SWOT Analysis is a technique used to identify and analyze the strengths, weaknesses, opportunities, and threats associated with a program.

46. Question: What is the primary goal of program resource management?

A) To track program schedule performance

B) To allocate resources to program activities efficiently

C) To manage program finances

D) To ensure program compliance with regulations

Answer: B) To allocate resources to program activities efficiently

Explanation: Program resource management focuses on allocating resources to program activities efficiently to meet program objectives.

47. Question: Which program management approach emphasizes a flexible, adaptive approach to changing requirements?

A) Traditional Program Management

B) Waterfall Program Management

C) Adaptive Program Management

D) Lean Program Management

Answer: C) Adaptive Program Management

Explanation: Adaptive Program Management emphasizes flexibility and adaptability to changing requirements and conditions.

48. Question: What is the primary purpose of a Program Dependency Matrix?

A) To allocate resources to program activities

B) To visualize program benefits

C) To identify and manage interdependencies between program components

D) To document program risks

Answer: C) To identify and manage interdependencies between program components

Explanation: A Program Dependency Matrix is used to identify and manage interdependencies between program components and activities.

49. Question: Which program management framework is known for its focus on governance, roles, and processes in program management?

A) SAFe (Scaled Agile Framework)

B) PRINCE2 (Projects IN Controlled Environments)

C) PMBOK (Project Management Body of Knowledge)

D) MSP (Managing Successful Programmes)

Answer: D) MSP (Managing Successful Programmes)

Explanation: MSP is known for its focus on governance, roles, and processes in program management.

50. Question: In program management, what is the primary purpose of a Program Schedule Management Plan?

A) To allocate resources to program activities

B) To visualize program benefits

C) To outline how program schedules will be developed, monitored, and controlled

D) To track program financial performance

Answer: C) To outline how program schedules will be developed, monitored, and controlled

Explanation: A Program Schedule Management Plan outlines how program schedules will be developed, monitored, and controlled throughout the program.

51. Question: Which program management approach emphasizes delivering value incrementally and frequently, with a focus on customer collaboration?

A) Agile Program Management

B) Traditional Program Management

C) Lean Program Management

D) Waterfall Program Management

Answer: A) Agile Program Management

Explanation: Agile Program Management focuses on delivering value incrementally and frequently, with a strong emphasis on customer collaboration and responding to change.

52. Question: What is the primary role of a Program Management Office (PMO) in program management?

A) To manage program finances

B) To provide administrative support to program managers

C) To oversee individual projects within the program

D) To support program managers and provide guidance and governance

Answer: D) To support program managers and provide guidance and governance

Explanation: The PMO's primary role in program management is to support program managers and provide guidance and governance to ensure program success.

53. Question: What is the primary focus of program benefits realization management?

A) To allocate resources to program activities

B) To track program schedule performance

C) To ensure that program benefits are achieved and sustained

D) To manage program risks

Answer: C) To ensure that program benefits are achieved and sustained

Explanation: Program benefits realization management focuses on ensuring that program benefits are achieved and sustained over time.

54. Question: In program management, what does the term "Dependency Analysis" refer to?

A) A technique for estimating program durations

B) A process for identifying and managing program dependencies

C) A method for documenting program risks

D) A tool for tracking program financial performance

Answer: B) A process for identifying and managing program dependencies

Explanation: Dependency Analysis is a process used to identify and manage program dependencies, ensuring that activities are sequenced appropriately.

55. Question: What is the primary goal of program stakeholder communication?

A) To allocate resources to program activities

B) To track program schedule performance

C) To provide relevant and timely information to program stakeholders

D) To manage program finances

Answer: C) To provide relevant and timely information to program stakeholders

Explanation: Program stakeholder communication aims to provide relevant and timely information to program stakeholders to keep them informed and engaged.

56. Question: Which program management approach is best suited for highly uncertain and complex programs with evolving requirements?

A) Traditional Program Management

B) Waterfall Program Management

C) Adaptive Program Management

D) Lean Program Management

Answer: C) Adaptive Program Management

Explanation: Adaptive Program Management is well-suited for highly uncertain and complex programs with evolving requirements.

57. Question: What is the primary purpose of a Program Issue Log?

A) To allocate resources to program activities

B) To visualize program benefits

C) To document and track program issues and their resolution

D) To assess program risks

Answer: C) To document and track program issues and their resolution

Explanation: A Program Issue Log is used to document and track program issues and their resolution, ensuring that they are addressed effectively.

58. Question: Which program management role is responsible for championing the program and advocating for its success?

A) Program Manager

B) Program Sponsor

C) Program Coordinator

D) Program Governance Board

Answer: B) Program Sponsor

Explanation: The Program Sponsor is responsible for championing the program and advocating for its success within the organization.

59. Question: In program management, what does the term "Program Risk Appetite" refer to?

A) The willingness to accept program risks

B) The program's budget allocation

C) The timeline for program delivery

D) The program's stakeholder engagement strategy

Answer: A) The willingness to accept program risks

Explanation: Program Risk Appetite refers to the organization's or program's willingness to accept and tolerate certain levels of risk.

60. Question: What is the primary purpose of a Program Closure Report?

A) To document program risks

B) To assess the realization of program benefits

C) To track program schedule performance

D) To create a detailed program budget

Answer: B) To assess the realization of program benefits

Explanation: A Program Closure Report assesses the realization of program benefits against expected outcomes, summarizing the program's achievements.

61. Question: What is the primary purpose of a Program Risk Register?

A) To allocate resources to program activities

B) To document program benefits

C) To identify and assess program risks

D) To track program schedule performance

Answer: C) To identify and assess program risks

Explanation: A Program Risk Register is used to identify and assess program risks that may impact program success.

62. Question: In program management, what does the term "Program Dependency Matrix" refer to?

A) A visual representation of program stakeholders

B) A tool for tracking program finances

C) A process for managing program dependencies

D) A document outlining program governance principles

Answer: C) A process for managing program dependencies

Explanation: A Program Dependency Matrix is used to manage program dependencies between various program components and activities.

63. Question: Which program management role is responsible for ensuring that program activities are aligned with organizational strategy?

A) Program Manager

B) Program Sponsor

C) Program Governance Board

D) Program Coordinator

Answer: B) Program Sponsor

Explanation: The Program Sponsor is responsible for ensuring that program activities align with organizational strategy and goals.

64. Question: What is the primary purpose of a Program Quality Management Plan?

A) To allocate resources to program activities

B) To visualize program benefits

C) To outline how program quality will be managed and assured

D) To track program financial performance

Answer: C) To outline how program quality will be managed and assured

Explanation: A Program Quality Management Plan outlines how program quality will be managed and assured throughout the program.

65. Question: Which program management approach is characterized by a focus on eliminating waste and maximizing value for the customer?

A) Agile Program Management

B) Traditional Program Management

C) Lean Program Management

D) Waterfall Program Management

Answer: C) Lean Program Management

Explanation: Lean Program Management focuses on eliminating waste and maximizing value, particularly for the customer.

66. Question: What is the primary goal of program stakeholder analysis?

A) To allocate resources to program activities

B) To track program schedule performance

C) To identify and understand the interests and influence of program stakeholders

D) To create a detailed program budget

Answer: C) To identify and understand the interests and influence of program stakeholders

Explanation: Program stakeholder analysis aims to identify and understand the interests and influence of program stakeholders.

67. Question: In program management, what does the term "Value Stream Mapping" refer to?

A) A visual representation of program components

B) A technique for assessing program risks

C) A process for identifying and optimizing the flow of value in a program

D) A method for tracking program schedule performance

Answer: C) A process for identifying and optimizing the flow of value in a program

Explanation: Value Stream Mapping is a process used to identify and optimize the flow of value across program activities and processes.

68. Question: What is the primary purpose of a Program Business Case?

A) To allocate resources to program activities

B) To visualize program benefits

C) To outline the program's high-level objectives and expected benefits

D) To track program financial performance

Answer: C) To outline the program's high-level objectives and expected benefits

Explanation: A Program Business Case outlines the program's high-level objectives and expected benefits to support decision-making.

69. Question: Which program management framework emphasizes a standardized approach to project and program management processes?

A) PRINCE2 (Projects IN Controlled Environments)

B) SAFe (Scaled Agile Framework)

C) PMBOK (Project Management Body of Knowledge)

D) MSP (Managing Successful Programmes)

Answer: A) PRINCE2 (Projects IN Controlled Environments)

Explanation: PRINCE2 emphasizes a standardized approach to project and program management processes.

70. Question: In program management, what does the term "Program Governance Framework" refer to?

A) A visual representation of program stakeholders

B) A tool for tracking program finances

C) A document outlining program governance principles and policies

D) A process for managing program dependencies

Answer: C) A document outlining program governance principles and policies

Explanation: A Program Governance Framework is a document that outlines the principles and policies governing program governance.

71. Question: What is the primary goal of program resource management?

A) To track program schedule performance

B) To allocate resources to program activities efficiently

C) To manage program finances

D) To ensure program compliance with regulations

Answer: B) To allocate resources to program activities efficiently

Explanation: Program resource management focuses on allocating resources to program activities efficiently to meet program objectives.

72. Question: Which program management approach is best suited for situations where requirements are well-defined, and there is little uncertainty?

A) Agile Program Management

B) Waterfall Program Management

C) Lean Program Management

D) Adaptive Program Management

Answer: B) Waterfall Program Management

Explanation: Waterfall Program Management is most suitable when requirements are well-defined and there is minimal uncertainty in the program.

73. Question: What is the primary purpose of a Program Dependency Matrix?

A) To allocate resources to program activities

B) To visualize program benefits

C) To identify and manage interdependencies between program components

D) To document program risks

Answer: C) To identify and manage interdependencies between program components

Explanation: A Program Dependency Matrix is used to identify and manage interdependencies between program components and activities.

74. Question: Which program management role is responsible for championing the program and advocating for its success?

A) Program Manager

B) Program Sponsor

C) Program Coordinator

D) Program Governance Board

Answer: B) Program Sponsor

Explanation: The Program Sponsor is responsible for championing the program and advocating for its success within the organization.

75. Question: In program management, what does the term "Program Risk Appetite" refer to?

A) The willingness to accept program risks

B) The program's budget allocation

C) The timeline for program delivery

D) The program's stakeholder engagement strategy

Answer: A) The willingness to accept program risks

Explanation: Program Risk Appetite refers to the organization's or program's willingness to accept and tolerate certain levels of risk.

76. Question: What is the primary goal of program stakeholder communication?

A) To allocate resources to program activities

B) To track program schedule performance

C) To provide relevant and timely information to program stakeholders

D) To manage program finances

Answer: C) To provide relevant and timely information to program stakeholders

Explanation: Program stakeholder communication aims to provide relevant and timely information to program stakeholders to keep them informed and engaged.

77. Question: Which program management approach emphasizes delivering value incrementally and frequently, with a focus on customer collaboration?

A) Agile Program Management

B) Traditional Program Management

C) Lean Program Management

D) Waterfall Program Management

Answer: A) Agile Program Management

Explanation: Agile Program Management focuses on delivering value incrementally and frequently, with a strong emphasis on customer collaboration and responding to change.

78. Question: What is the primary role of a Program Management Office (PMO) in program management?

A) To manage program finances

B) To provide administrative support to program managers

C) To oversee individual projects within the program

D) To support program managers and provide guidance and governance

Answer: D) To support program managers and provide guidance and governance

Explanation: The PMO's primary role in program management is to support program managers and provide guidance and governance to ensure program success.

79. Question: What is the primary focus of program benefits realization management?

A) To allocate resources to program activities

B) To track program schedule performance

C) To ensure that program benefits are achieved and sustained

D) To manage program risks

Answer: C) To ensure that program benefits are achieved and sustained

Explanation: Program benefits realization management focuses on ensuring that program benefits are achieved and sustained over time.

80. Question: In program management, what does the term "Dependency Analysis" refer to?

A) A technique for estimating program durations

B) A process for identifying and managing program dependencies

C) A method for documenting program risks

D) A tool for tracking program financial performance

Answer: B) A process for identifying and managing program dependencies

Explanation: Dependency Analysis is a process used to identify and manage program dependencies, ensuring that activities are sequenced appropriately.

81. Question: What is the primary purpose of a Program Benefits Realization Plan?

A) To allocate resources to program activities

B) To visualize program benefits

C) To outline how program benefits will be realized and measured

D) To track program financial performance

Answer: C) To outline how program benefits will be realized and measured

Explanation: A Program Benefits Realization Plan outlines how program benefits will be realized and measured, ensuring alignment with program objectives.

82. Question: Which program management role is responsible for ensuring that program activities adhere to established policies and procedures?

A) Program Manager

B) Program Sponsor

C) Program Governance Board

D) Program Coordinator

Answer: C) Program Governance Board

Explanation: The Program Governance Board is responsible for ensuring program activities adhere to established policies and procedures.

83. Question: In program management, what does the term "Program Roadmap" refer to?

A) A visual representation of program stakeholders

B) A tool for tracking program finances

C) A high-level plan outlining key program milestones and deliverables

D) A process for managing program dependencies

Answer: C) A high-level plan outlining key program milestones and deliverables

Explanation: A Program Roadmap is a high-level plan that outlines key program milestones and deliverables, providing a strategic view of the program.

84. Question: What is the primary purpose of a Program Issue Log?

A) To allocate resources to program activities

B) To document program benefits

C) To identify and track program issues and their resolution

D) To assess program risks

Answer: C) To identify and track program issues and their resolution

Explanation: A Program Issue Log is used to identify and track program issues and their resolution, ensuring they are addressed effectively.

85. Question: Which program management technique involves ranking program projects based on their strategic importance and alignment with organizational goals?

A) Program Evaluation and Review Technique (PERT)

B) Earned Value Management (EVM)

C) Program Prioritization

D) Critical Chain Method (CCM)

Answer: C) Program Prioritization

Explanation: Program Prioritization involves ranking program projects based on their strategic importance and alignment with organizational goals.

86. Question: What is the primary goal of program financial management?

A) To track program schedule performance

B) To allocate resources to program activities efficiently

C) To ensure program compliance with regulations

D) To manage program finances efficiently and effectively

Answer: D) To manage program finances efficiently and effectively

Explanation: Program financial management focuses on managing program finances efficiently and effectively to achieve program objectives.

87. Question: Which program management framework emphasizes a holistic approach to managing business change?

A) PRINCE2 (Projects IN Controlled Environments)

B) MSP (Managing Successful Programmes)

C) PMBOK (Project Management Body of Knowledge)

D) SAFe (Scaled Agile Framework)

Answer: B) MSP (Managing Successful Programmes)

Explanation: MSP emphasizes a holistic approach to managing business change through programs.

88. Question: In program management, what does the term "Program Risk Tolerance" refer to?

A) The willingness to accept program risks

B) The program's budget allocation

C) The timeline for program delivery

D) The program's stakeholder engagement strategy

Answer: A) The willingness to accept program risks

Explanation: Program Risk Tolerance refers to the organization's or program's willingness to accept and tolerate certain levels of risk.

89. Question: What is the primary purpose of a Program Closure Report?

A) To allocate resources to program activities

B) To assess the realization of program benefits against expected outcomes

C) To track program financial performance

D) To create a detailed program budget

Answer: B) To assess the realization of program benefits against expected outcomes

Explanation: A Program Closure Report assesses the realization of program benefits against expected outcomes, summarizing the program's achievements.

90. Question: Which program management approach emphasizes delivering value incrementally and frequently, with a focus on customer collaboration?

A) Agile Program Management

B) Traditional Program Management

C) Lean Program Management

D) Waterfall Program Management

Answer: A) Agile Program Management

Explanation: Agile Program Management focuses on delivering value incrementally and frequently, with a strong emphasis on customer collaboration and responding to change.

91. Question: What is the primary role of a Program Management Office (PMO) in program management?

A) To manage program finances

B) To provide administrative support to program managers

C) To oversee individual projects within the program

D) To support program managers and provide guidance and governance

Answer: D) To support program managers and provide guidance and governance

Explanation: The PMO's primary role in program management is to support program managers and provide guidance and governance to ensure program success.

92. Question: In program management, what does the term "Dependency Analysis" refer to?

A) A technique for estimating program durations

B) A process for identifying and managing program dependencies

C) A method for documenting program risks

D) A tool for tracking program financial performance

Answer: B) A process for

Explanation: Dependency Analysis in program management refers to the process of identifying and managing program dependencies, ensuring that activities are sequenced appropriately to achieve program goals.

93. Question: What is the primary goal of program stakeholder communication?

A) To allocate resources to program activities

B) To track program schedule performance

C) To provide relevant and timely information to program stakeholders

D) To manage program finances

Answer: C) To provide relevant and timely information to program stakeholders

Explanation: The primary goal of program stakeholder communication is to provide relevant and timely information to program stakeholders, ensuring they are well-informed and engaged in program activities.

94. Question: Which program management approach is best suited for highly uncertain and complex programs with evolving requirements?

A) Traditional Program Management

B) Waterfall Program Management

C) Adaptive Program Management

D) Lean Program Management

Answer: C) Adaptive Program Management

Explanation: Adaptive Program Management is well-suited for highly uncertain and complex programs with evolving requirements, as it allows for flexibility and adaptation.

95. Question: What is the primary purpose of a Program Issue Log?

A) To allocate resources to program activities

B) To visualize program benefits

C) To document and track program issues and their resolution

D) To assess program risks

Answer: C) To document and track program issues and their resolution

Explanation: A Program Issue Log is used to document and track program issues and their resolution, ensuring that they are addressed effectively.

96. Question: Which program management role is responsible for championing the program and advocating for its success?

A) Program Manager

B) Program Sponsor

C) Program Coordinator

D) Program Governance Board

Answer: B) Program Sponsor

Explanation: The Program Sponsor is responsible for championing the program and advocating for its success within the organization.

97. Question: In program management, what does the term "Program Risk Appetite" refer to?

A) The willingness to accept program risks

B) The program's budget allocation

C) The timeline for program delivery

D) The program's stakeholder engagement strategy

Answer: A) The willingness to accept program risks

Explanation: Program Risk Appetite refers to the organization's or program's willingness to accept and tolerate certain levels of risk.

98. Question: What is the primary purpose of a Program Closure Report?

A) To allocate resources to program activities

B) To assess the realization of program benefits against expected outcomes

C) To track program financial performance

D) To create a detailed program budget

Answer: B) To assess the realization of program benefits against expected outcomes

Explanation: A Program Closure Report assesses the realization of program benefits against expected outcomes, summarizing the program's achievements.

99. Question: In program management, what is the primary purpose of a Program Evaluation and Review Technique (PERT)?

A) To allocate resources to program activities

B) To visualize program benefits

C) To estimate program durations based on optimistic, pessimistic, and most likely scenarios

D) To track program financial performance

Answer: C) To estimate program durations based on optimistic, pessimistic, and most likely scenarios

Explanation: PERT is used in program management to estimate program durations based on optimistic, pessimistic, and most likely scenarios, helping with scheduling and planning.

100. Question: What is the primary focus of program stakeholder analysis?

A) To allocate resources to program activities

B) To track program schedule performance

C) To identify and understand the interests and influence of program stakeholders

D) To create a detailed program budget

Answer: C) To identify and understand the interests and influence of program stakeholders

Explanation: Program stakeholder analysis aims to identify and understand the interests and influence of program stakeholders, helping in effective stakeholder management.

101. Question: What is the primary purpose of a Program Benefits Dependency Map?

A) To allocate resources to program activities

B) To visualize program benefits

C) To identify dependencies between program benefits

D) To track program schedule performance

Answer: C) To identify dependencies between program benefits

Explanation: A Benefits Dependency Map helps identify dependencies between program benefits, helping to understand how they relate to one another.

102. Question: Which program management role is responsible for ensuring that program deliverables meet quality standards?

A) Program Manager

B) Program Sponsor

C) Program Quality Assurance Manager

D) Program Coordinator

Answer: C) Program Quality Assurance Manager

Explanation: The Program Quality Assurance Manager is responsible for ensuring that program deliverables meet quality standards.

103. Question: In program management, what does the term "Program Governance Framework" refer to?

A) A document outlining program governance principles and policies

B) The hierarchy of program governance roles

C) The program's timeline and milestones

D) The program's budget allocation

Answer: A) A document outlining program governance principles and policies

Explanation: A Program Governance Framework is a document that outlines the principles and policies governing program governance.

104. Question: What is the primary purpose of a Program Risk Response Plan?

A) To document program risks

B) To outline the program's risk mitigation strategies

C) To allocate resources to program activities

D) To track program schedule performance

Answer: B) To outline the program's risk mitigation strategies

Explanation: A Program Risk Response Plan outlines the strategies and actions to mitigate identified program risks.

105. Question: Which program management technique involves identifying and analyzing the strengths, weaknesses, opportunities, and threats associated with a program?

A) SWOT Analysis

B) Earned Value Management (EVM)

C) Value Stream Mapping

D) Critical Chain Method (CCM)

Answer: A) SWOT Analysis

Explanation: SWOT Analysis is a technique used to identify and analyze the strengths, weaknesses, opportunities, and threats associated with a program.

106. Question: What is the primary goal of program resource management?

A) To track program schedule performance

B) To allocate resources to program activities efficiently

C) To manage program finances

D) To ensure program compliance with regulations

Answer: B) To allocate resources to program activities efficiently

Explanation: Program resource management focuses on allocating resources to program activities efficiently to meet program objectives.

107. Question: Which program management approach emphasizes a flexible, adaptive approach to changing requirements?

A) Traditional Program Management

B) Waterfall Program Management

C) Adaptive Program Management

D) Lean Program Management

Answer: C) Adaptive Program Management

Explanation: Adaptive Program Management emphasizes flexibility and adaptability to changing requirements and conditions.

108. Question: What is the primary purpose of a Program Dependency Matrix?

A) To allocate resources to program activities

B) To visualize program benefits

C) To identify and manage interdependencies between program components

D) To document program risks

Answer: C) To identify and manage interdependencies between program components

Explanation: A Program Dependency Matrix is used to identify and manage interdependencies between program components and activities.

109. Question: Which program management framework is known for its focus on governance, roles, and processes in program management?

A) SAFe (Scaled Agile Framework)

B) PRINCE2 (Projects IN Controlled Environments)

C) PMBOK (Project Management Body of Knowledge)

D) MSP (Managing Successful Programmes)

Answer: D) MSP (Managing Successful Programmes)

Explanation: MSP is known for its focus on governance, roles, and processes in program management.

110. Question: In program management, what does the term "Program Schedule Management Plan" refer to?

A) A visual representation of the program schedule

B) A technique for estimating program risks

C) A process for identifying and optimizing the flow of value in a program

D) A method for documenting program benefits

Answer: A) A visual representation of the program schedule

Explanation: A Program Schedule Management Plan includes a visual representation of the program schedule, outlining key milestones and activities.

111. Question: Which program management approach emphasizes delivering value incrementally and frequently, with a focus on customer collaboration?

A) Agile Program Management

B) Traditional Program Management

C) Lean Program Management

D) Waterfall Program Management

Answer: A) Agile Program Management

Explanation: Agile Program Management focuses on delivering value incrementally and frequently, with a strong emphasis on customer collaboration and responding to change.

112. Question: What is the primary role of a Program Management Office (PMO) in program management?

A) To manage program finances

B) To provide administrative support to program managers

C) To oversee individual projects within the program

D) To support program managers and provide guidance and governance

Answer: D) To support program managers and provide guidance and governance

Explanation: The PMO's primary role in program management is to support program managers and provide guidance and governance to ensure program success.

113. Question: What is the primary focus of program benefits realization management?

A) To allocate resources to program activities

B) To track program schedule performance

C) To ensure that program benefits are achieved and sustained

D) To manage program risks

Answer: C) To ensure that program benefits are achieved and sustained

Explanation: Program benefits realization management focuses on ensuring that program benefits are achieved and sustained over time.

114. Question: In program management, what does the term "Dependency Analysis" refer to?

A) A technique for estimating program durations

B) A process for identifying and managing program dependencies

C) A method for documenting program risks

D) A tool for tracking program financial performance

Answer: B) A process for identifying and managing program dependencies

Explanation: Dependency Analysis is a process used to identify and manage program dependencies, ensuring that activities are sequenced appropriately to achieve program goals.

115. Question: What is the primary goal of program stakeholder communication?

A) To allocate resources to program activities

B) To track program schedule performance

C) To provide relevant and timely information to program stakeholders

D) To manage program finances

Answer: C) To provide relevant and timely information to program stakeholders

Explanation: The primary goal of program stakeholder communication is to provide relevant and timely information to program stakeholders, ensuring they are well-informed and engaged in program activities.

116. Question: Which program management approach is best suited for situations where requirements are well-defined, and there is little uncertainty?

A) Agile Program Management

B) Waterfall Program Management

C) Lean Program Management

D) Adaptive Program Management

Answer: B) Waterfall Program Management

Explanation: Waterfall Program Management is most suitable when requirements are well-defined, and there is minimal uncertainty in the program.

117. Question: What is the primary purpose of a Program Dependency Matrix?

A) To allocate resources to program activities

B) To visualize program benefits

C) To identify and manage interdependencies between program components

D) To document program risks

Answer: C) To identify and manage interdependencies between program components

Explanation: A Program Dependency Matrix is used to identify and manage interdependencies between program components and activities.

118. Question: Which program management role is responsible for championing the program and advocating for its success?

A) Program Manager

B) Program Sponsor

C) Program Coordinator

D) Program Governance Board

Answer: B) Program Sponsor

Explanation: The Program Sponsor is responsible for championing the program and advocating for its success within the organization.

119. Question: In program management, what does the term "Program Risk Appetite" refer to?

A) The willingness to accept program risks

B) The program's budget allocation

C) The timeline for program delivery

D) The program's stakeholder engagement strategy

Answer: A) The willingness to accept program risks

Explanation: Program Risk Appetite refers to the organization's or program's willingness to accept and tolerate certain levels of risk.

120. Question: What is the primary purpose of a Program Closure Report?

A) To allocate resources to program activities

B) To assess the realization of program benefits against expected outcomes

C) To track program financial performance

D) To create a detailed program budget

Answer: B) To assess the realization of program benefits against expected outcomes

Explanation: A Program Closure Report assesses the realization of program benefits against expected outcomes, summarizing the program's achievements.

121. Question: What is the primary purpose of a Program Quality Assurance Plan?

A) To allocate resources to program activities

B) To visualize program benefits

C) To outline how program quality will be assured

D) To track program schedule performance

Answer: C) To outline how program quality will be assured

Explanation: A Program Quality Assurance Plan outlines how program quality will be assured throughout the program's lifecycle.

122. Question: Which program management role is responsible for ensuring that program activities align with organizational strategy and goals?

A) Program Manager

B) Program Sponsor

C) Program Coordinator

D) Program Governance Board

Answer: B) Program Sponsor

Explanation: The Program Sponsor is responsible for ensuring that program activities align with organizational strategy and goals.

123. Question: In program management, what does the term "Program Roadmap" refer to?

A) A visual representation of program stakeholders

B) A tool for tracking program finances

C) A high-level plan outlining key program milestones and deliverables

D) A process for managing program dependencies

Answer: C) A high-level plan outlining key program milestones and deliverables

Explanation: A Program Roadmap is a high-level plan that outlines key program milestones and deliverables, providing a strategic view of the program.

124. Question: What is the primary purpose of a Program Issue Log?

A) To allocate resources to program activities

B) To document program benefits

C) To identify and track program issues and their resolution

D) To assess program risks

Answer: C) To identify and track program issues and their resolution

Explanation: A Program Issue Log is used to identify and track program issues and their resolution, ensuring they are addressed effectively.

125. Question: Which program management technique involves ranking program projects based on their strategic importance and alignment with organizational goals?

A) Program Evaluation and Review Technique (PERT)

B) Earned Value Management (EVM)

C) Program Prioritization

D) Critical Chain Method (CCM)

Answer: C) Program Prioritization

Explanation: Program Prioritization involves ranking program projects based on their strategic importance and alignment with organizational goals.

126. Question: What is the primary goal of program resource management?

A) To track program schedule performance

B) To allocate resources to program activities efficiently

C) To manage program finances

D) To ensure program compliance with regulations

Answer: B) To allocate resources to program activities efficiently

Explanation: Program resource management focuses on allocating resources to program activities efficiently to meet program objectives.

127. Question: Which program management framework emphasizes a holistic approach to managing business change through programs?

A) PRINCE2 (Projects IN Controlled Environments)

B) MSP (Managing Successful Programmes)

C) PMBOK (Project Management Body of Knowledge)

D) SAFe (Scaled Agile Framework)

Answer: B) MSP (Managing Successful Programmes)

Explanation: MSP emphasizes a holistic approach to managing business change through programs.

128. Question: In program management, what does the term "Program Risk Tolerance" refer to?

A) The willingness to accept program risks

B) The program's budget allocation

C) The timeline for program delivery

D) The program's stakeholder engagement strategy

Answer: A) The willingness to accept program risks

Explanation: Program Risk Tolerance refers to the organization's or program's willingness to accept and tolerate certain levels of risk.

129. Question: What is the primary purpose of a Program Closure Report?

A) To allocate resources to program activities

B) To assess the realization of program benefits against expected outcomes

C) To track program financial performance

D) To create a detailed program budget

Answer: B) To assess the realization of program benefits against expected outcomes

Explanation: A Program Closure Report assesses the realization of program benefits against expected outcomes, summarizing the program's achievements.

130. Question: Which program management approach emphasizes delivering value incrementally and frequently, with a focus on customer collaboration?

A) Agile Program Management

B) Traditional Program Management

C) Lean Program Management

D) Waterfall Program Management

Answer: A) Agile Program Management

Explanation: Agile Program Management focuses on delivering value incrementally and frequently, with a strong emphasis on customer collaboration and responding to change.

131. Question: What is the primary role of a Program Management Office (PMO) in program management?

A) To manage program finances

B) To provide administrative support to program managers

C) To oversee individual projects within the program

D) To support program managers and provide guidance and governance

Answer: D) To support program managers and provide guidance and governance

Explanation: The PMO's primary role in program management is to support program managers and provide guidance and governance to ensure program success.

132. Question: In program management, what does the term "Dependency Analysis" refer to?

A) A technique for estimating program durations

B) A process for identifying and managing program dependencies

C) A method for documenting program risks

D) A tool for tracking program financial performance

Answer: B) A process for identifying and managing program dependencies

Explanation: Dependency Analysis is a process used to identify and manage program dependencies, ensuring that activities are sequenced appropriately to achieve program goals.

133. Question: What is the primary goal of program stakeholder communication?

A) To allocate resources to program activities

B) To track program schedule performance

C) To provide relevant and timely information to program stakeholders

D) To manage program finances

Answer: C) To provide relevant and timely information to program stakeholders

Explanation: The primary goal of program stakeholder communication is to provide relevant and timely information to program stakeholders, ensuring they are well-informed and engaged in program activities.

134. Question: Which program management approach is best suited for highly uncertain and complex programs with evolving requirements?

A) Traditional Program Management

B) Waterfall Program Management

C) Adaptive Program Management

D) Lean Program Management

Answer: C) Adaptive Program Management

Explanation: Adaptive Program Management is well-suited for highly uncertain and complex programs with evolving requirements, as it allows for flexibility and adaptation.

135. Question: What is the primary purpose of a Program Issue Log?

A) To allocate resources to program activities

B) To visualize program benefits

C) To document and track program issues and their resolution

D) To assess program risks

Answer: C) To document and track program issues and their resolution

Explanation: A Program Issue Log is used to document and track program issues and their resolution, ensuring that they are addressed effectively.

136. Question: Which program management role is responsible for championing the program and advocating for its success?

A) Program Manager

B) Program Sponsor

C) Program Coordinator

D) Program Governance Board

Answer: B) Program Sponsor

Explanation: The Program Sponsor is responsible for championing the program and advocating for its success within the organization.

137. Question: In program management, what does the term "Program Risk Appetite" refer to?

A) The willingness to accept program risks

B) The program's budget allocation

C) The timeline for program delivery

D) The program's stakeholder engagement strategy

Answer: A) The willingness to accept program risks

Explanation: Program Risk Appetite refers to the organization's or program's willingness to accept and tolerate certain levels of risk.

138. Question: What is the primary purpose of a Program Closure Report?

A) To allocate resources to program activities

B) To assess the realization of program benefits against expected outcomes

C) To track program financial performance

D) To create a detailed program budget

Answer: B) To assess the realization of program benefits against expected outcomes

Explanation: A Program Closure Report assesses the realization of program benefits against expected outcomes, summarizing the program's achievements.

139. Question: In program management, what is the primary purpose of a Program Evaluation and Review Technique (PERT)?

A) To allocate resources to program activities

B) To visualize program benefits

C) To estimate program durations based on optimistic, pessimistic, and most likely scenarios

D) To track program financial performance

Answer: C) To estimate program durations based on optimistic, pessimistic, and most likely scenarios

Explanation: PERT is used in program management to estimate program durations based on optimistic, pessimistic, and most likely scenarios, helping with scheduling and planning.

140. Question: What is the primary focus of program stakeholder analysis?

A) To allocate resources to program activities

B) To track program schedule performance

C) To identify and understand the interests and influence of program stakeholders

D) To create a detailed program budget

Answer: C) To identify and understand the interests and influence of program stakeholders

Explanation: Program stakeholder analysis aims to identify and understand the interests and influence of program stakeholders, helping in effective stakeholder management.

141. Question: What is the primary purpose of a Program Quality Assurance Plan?

A) To allocate resources to program activities

B) To visualize program benefits

C) To outline how program quality will be assured

D) To track program schedule performance

Answer: C) To outline how program quality will be assured

Explanation: A Program Quality Assurance Plan outlines how program quality will be assured throughout the program's lifecycle.

142. Question: Which program management role is responsible for ensuring that program activities align with organizational strategy and goals?

A) Program Manager

B) Program Sponsor

C) Program Coordinator

D) Program Governance Board

Answer: B) Program Sponsor

Explanation: The Program Sponsor is responsible for ensuring that program activities align with organizational strategy and goals.

143. Question: In program management, what does the term "Program Roadmap" refer to?

A) A visual representation of program stakeholders

B) A tool for tracking program finances

C) A high-level plan outlining key program milestones and deliverables

D) A process for managing program dependencies

Answer: C) A high-level plan outlining key program milestones and deliverables

Explanation: A Program Roadmap is a high-level plan that outlines key program milestones and deliverables, providing a strategic view of the program.

144. Question: What is the primary purpose of a Program Issue Log?

A) To allocate resources to program activities

B) To document program benefits

C) To identify and track program issues and their resolution

D) To assess program risks

Answer: C) To identify and track program issues and their resolution

Explanation: A Program Issue Log is used to identify and track program issues and their resolution, ensuring they are addressed effectively.

145. Question: Which program management technique involves ranking program projects based on their strategic importance and alignment with organizational goals?

A) Program Evaluation and Review Technique (PERT)
B) Earned Value Management (EVM)
C) Program Prioritization
D) Critical Chain Method (CCM)

Answer: C) Program Prioritization

Explanation: Program Prioritization involves ranking program projects based on their strategic importance and alignment with organizational goals.

146. Question: What is the primary goal of program resource management?

A) To track program schedule performance
B) To allocate resources to program activities efficiently
C) To manage program finances
D) To ensure program compliance with regulations

Answer: B) To allocate resources to program activities efficiently

Explanation: Program resource management focuses on allocating resources to program activities efficiently to meet program objectives.

147. Question: Which program management framework emphasizes a holistic approach to managing business change through programs?

A) PRINCE2 (Projects IN Controlled Environments)
B) MSP (Managing Successful Programmes)
C) PMBOK (Project Management Body of Knowledge)
D) SAFe (Scaled Agile Framework)

Answer: B) MSP (Managing Successful Programmes)

Explanation: MSP emphasizes a holistic approach to managing business change through programs.

148. Question: In program management, what does the term "Program Risk Tolerance" refer to?

A) The willingness to accept program risks

B) The program's budget allocation

C) The timeline for program delivery

D) The program's stakeholder engagement strategy

Answer: A) The willingness to accept program risks

Explanation: Program Risk Tolerance refers to the organization's or program's willingness to accept and tolerate certain levels of risk.

149. Question: What is the primary purpose of a Program Closure Report?

A) To allocate resources to program activities

B) To assess the realization of program benefits against expected outcomes

C) To track program financial performance

D) To create a detailed program budget

Answer: B) To assess the realization of program benefits against expected outcomes

Explanation: A Program Closure Report assesses the realization of program benefits against expected outcomes, summarizing the program's achievements.

150. Question: Which program management approach emphasizes delivering value incrementally and frequently, with a focus on customer collaboration?

A) Agile Program Management

B) Traditional Program Management

C) Lean Program Management

D) Waterfall Program Management

Answer: A) Agile Program Management

Explanation: Agile Program Management focuses on delivering value incrementally and frequently, with a strong emphasis on customer collaboration and responding to change.

151. Question: What is the primary role of a Program Management Office (PMO) in program management?

A) To manage program finances

B) To provide administrative support to program managers

C) To oversee individual projects within the program

D) To support program managers and provide guidance and governance

Answer: D) To support program managers and provide guidance and governance

Explanation: The PMO's primary role in program management is to support program managers and provide guidance and governance to ensure program success.

152. Question: In program management, what does the term "Dependency Analysis" refer to?

A) A technique for estimating program durations

B) A process for identifying and managing program dependencies

C) A method for documenting program risks

D) A tool for tracking program financial performance

Answer: B) A process for identifying and managing program dependencies

Explanation: Dependency Analysis is a process used to identify and manage program dependencies, ensuring that activities are sequenced appropriately to achieve program goals.

153. Question: What is the primary goal of program stakeholder communication?

A) To allocate resources to program activities

B) To track program schedule performance

C) To provide relevant and timely information to program stakeholders

D) To manage program finances

Answer: C) To provide relevant and timely information to program stakeholders

Explanation: The primary goal of program stakeholder communication is to provide relevant and timely information to program stakeholders, ensuring they are well-informed and engaged in program activities.

154. Question: Which program management approach is best suited for highly uncertain and complex programs with evolving requirements?

A) Traditional Program Management

B) Waterfall Program Management

C) Adaptive Program Management

D) Lean Program Management

Answer: C) Adaptive Program Management

Explanation: Adaptive Program Management is well-suited for highly uncertain and complex programs with evolving requirements, as it allows for flexibility and adaptation.

155. Question: What is the primary purpose of a Program Issue Log?

A) To allocate resources to program activities

B) To visualize program benefits

C) To document and track program issues and their resolution

D) To assess program risks

Answer: C) To document and track program issues and their resolution

Explanation: A Program Issue Log is used to document and track program issues and their resolution, ensuring they are addressed effectively.

156. Question: Which program management role is responsible for championing the program and advocating for its success?

A) Program Manager

B) Program Sponsor

C) Program Coordinator

D) Program Governance Board

Answer: B) Program Sponsor

Explanation: The Program Sponsor is responsible for championing the program and advocating for its success within the organization.

157. Question: In program management, what does the term "Program Risk Appetite" refer to?

A) The willingness to accept program risks

B) The program's budget allocation

C) The timeline for program delivery

D) The program's stakeholder engagement strategy

Answer: A) The willingness to accept program risks

Explanation: Program Risk Appetite refers to the organization's or program's willingness to accept and tolerate certain levels of risk.

158. Question: What is the primary purpose of a Program Closure Report?

A) To allocate resources to program activities

B) To assess the realization of program benefits against expected outcomes

C) To track program financial performance

D) To create a detailed program budget

Answer: B) To assess the realization of program benefits against expected outcomes

Explanation: A Program Closure Report assesses the realization of program benefits against expected outcomes, summarizing the program's achievements.

159. Question: In program management, what is the primary purpose of a Program Evaluation and Review Technique (PERT)?

A) To allocate resources to program activities

B) To visualize program benefits

C) To estimate program durations based on optimistic, pessimistic, and most likely scenarios

D) To track program financial performance

Answer: C) To estimate program durations based on optimistic, pessimistic, and most likely scenarios

Explanation: PERT is used in program management to estimate program durations based on optimistic, pessimistic, and most likely scenarios, helping with scheduling and planning.

160. Question: What is the primary focus of program stakeholder analysis?

A) To allocate resources to program activities

B) To track program schedule performance

C) To identify and understand the interests and influence of program stakeholders

D) To create a detailed program budget

Answer: C) To identify and understand the interests and influence of program stakeholders

Explanation: Program stakeholder analysis aims to identify and understand the interests and influence of program stakeholders, helping in effective stakeholder management.

161. Question: What is the primary purpose of a Program Quality Assurance Plan?

A) To allocate resources to program activities

B) To visualize program benefits

C) To outline how program quality will be assured

D) To track program schedule performance

Answer: C) To outline how program quality will be assured

Explanation: A Program Quality Assurance Plan outlines how program quality will be assured throughout the program's lifecycle.

162. Question: Which program management role is responsible for ensuring that program activities align with organizational strategy and goals?

A) Program Manager

B) Program Sponsor

C) Program Coordinator

D) Program Governance Board

Answer: B) Program Sponsor

Explanation: The Program Sponsor is responsible for ensuring that program activities align with organizational strategy and goals.

163. Question: In program management, what does the term "Program Roadmap" refer to?

A) A visual representation of program stakeholders

B) A tool for tracking program finances

C) A high-level plan outlining key program milestones and deliverables

D) A process for managing program dependencies

Answer: C) A high-level plan outlining key program milestones and deliverables

Explanation: A Program Roadmap is a high-level plan that outlines key program milestones and deliverables, providing a strategic view of the program.

164. Question: What is the primary purpose of a Program Issue Log?

A) To allocate resources to program activities

B) To document program benefits

C) To identify and track program issues and their resolution

D) To assess program risks

Answer: C) To identify and track program issues and their resolution

Explanation: A Program Issue Log is used to identify and track program issues and their resolution, ensuring they are addressed effectively.

165. Question: Which program management technique involves ranking program projects based on their strategic importance and alignment with organizational goals?

A) Program Evaluation and Review Technique (PERT)

B) Earned Value Management (EVM)

C) Program Prioritization

D) Critical Chain Method (CCM)

Answer: C) Program Prioritization

Explanation: Program Prioritization involves ranking program projects based on their strategic importance and alignment with organizational goals.

166. Question: What is the primary goal of program resource management?

A) To track program schedule performance

B) To allocate resources to program activities efficiently

C) To manage program finances

D) To ensure program compliance with regulations

Answer: B) To allocate resources to program activities efficiently

Explanation: Program resource management focuses on allocating resources to program activities efficiently to meet program objectives.

167. Question: Which program management framework emphasizes a holistic approach to managing business change through programs?

A) PRINCE2 (Projects IN Controlled Environments)

B) MSP (Managing Successful Programmes)

C) PMBOK (Project Management Body of Knowledge)

D) SAFe (Scaled Agile Framework)

Answer: B) MSP (Managing Successful Programmes)

Explanation: MSP emphasizes a holistic approach to managing business change through programs.

168. Question: In program management, what does the term "Program Risk Tolerance" refer to?

A) The willingness to accept program risks

B) The program's budget allocation

C) The timeline for program delivery

D) The program's stakeholder engagement strategy

Answer: A) The willingness to accept program risks

Explanation: Program Risk Tolerance refers to the organization's or program's willingness to accept and tolerate certain levels of risk.

169. Question: What is the primary purpose of a Program Closure Report?

A) To allocate resources to program activities

B) To assess the realization of program benefits against expected outcomes

C) To track program financial performance

D) To create a detailed program budget

Answer: B) To assess the realization of program benefits against expected outcomes

Explanation: A Program Closure Report assesses the realization of program benefits against expected outcomes, summarizing the program's achievements.

170. Question: Which program management approach emphasizes delivering value incrementally and frequently, with a focus on customer collaboration?

A) Agile Program Management

B) Traditional Program Management

C) Lean Program Management

D) Waterfall Program Management

Answer: A) Agile Program Management

Explanation: Agile Program Management focuses on delivering value incrementally and frequently, with a strong emphasis on customer collaboration and responding to change.

PRACTICE TEST -2

171. Question: What is the primary role of a Program Management Office (PMO) in program management?

A) To manage program finances

B) To provide administrative support to program managers

C) To oversee individual projects within the program

D) To support program managers and provide guidance and governance

Answer: D) To support program managers and provide guidance and governance

Explanation: The PMO's primary role in program management is to support program managers and provide guidance and governance to ensure program success.

172. Question: In program management, what does the term "Dependency Analysis" refer to?

A) A technique for estimating program durations

B) A process for identifying and managing program dependencies

C) A method for documenting program risks

D) A tool for tracking program financial performance

Answer: B) A process for identifying and managing program dependencies

Explanation: Dependency Analysis is a process used to identify and manage program dependencies, ensuring that activities are sequenced appropriately to achieve program goals.

173. Question: What is the primary goal of program stakeholder communication?

A) To allocate resources to program activities

B) To track program schedule performance

C) To provide relevant and timely information to program stakeholders

D) To manage program finances

Answer: C) To provide relevant and timely information to program stakeholders

Explanation: The primary goal of program stakeholder communication is to provide relevant and timely information to program stakeholders, ensuring they are well-informed and engaged in program activities.

174. Question: Which program management approach is best suited for highly uncertain and complex programs with evolving requirements?

A) Traditional Program Management

B) Waterfall Program Management

C) Adaptive Program Management

D) Lean Program Management

Answer: C) Adaptive Program Management

Explanation: Adaptive Program Management is well-suited for highly uncertain and complex programs with evolving requirements, as it allows for flexibility and adaptation.

175. Question: What is the primary purpose of a Program Issue Log?

A) To allocate resources to program activities

B) To visualize program benefits

C) To document and track program issues and their resolution

D) To assess program risks

Answer: C) To document and track program issues and their resolution

Explanation: A Program Issue Log is used to document and track program issues and their resolution, ensuring that they are addressed effectively.

176. Question: Which program management role is responsible for championing the program and advocating for its success?

A) Program Manager

B) Program Sponsor

C) Program Coordinator

D) Program Governance Board

Answer: B) Program Sponsor

Explanation: The Program Sponsor is responsible for championing the program and advocating for its success within the organization.

177. Question: In program management, what does the term "Program Risk Appetite" refer to?

A) The willingness to accept program risks

B) The program's budget allocation

C) The timeline for program delivery

D) The program's stakeholder engagement strategy

Answer: A) The willingness to accept program risks

Explanation: Program Risk Appetite refers to the organization's or program's willingness to accept and tolerate certain levels of risk.

178. Question: What is the primary purpose of a Program Closure Report?

A) To allocate resources to program activities

B) To assess the realization of program benefits against expected outcomes

C) To track program financial performance

D) To create a detailed program budget

Answer: B) To assess the realization of program benefits against expected outcomes

Explanation: A Program Closure Report assesses the realization of program benefits against expected outcomes, summarizing the program's achievements.

179. Question: In program management, what is the primary purpose of a Program Evaluation and Review Technique (PERT)?

A) To allocate resources to program activities

B) To visualize program benefits

C) To estimate program durations based on optimistic, pessimistic, and most likely scenarios

D) To track program financial performance

Answer: C) To estimate program durations based on optimistic, pessimistic, and most likely scenarios

Explanation: PERT is used in program management to estimate program durations based on optimistic, pessimistic, and most likely scenarios, helping with scheduling and planning.

180. Question: What is the primary focus of program stakeholder analysis?

A) To allocate resources to program activities

B) To track program schedule performance

C) To identify and understand the interests and influence of program stakeholders

D) To create a detailed program budget

Answer: C) To identify and understand the interests and influence of program stakeholders

Explanation: Program stakeholder analysis aims to identify and understand the interests and influence of program stakeholders, helping in effective stakeholder management.

181. Question: What is the primary purpose of a Program Quality Assurance Plan?

A) To allocate resources to program activities

B) To visualize program benefits

C) To outline how program quality will be assured

D) To track program schedule performance

Answer: C) To outline how program quality will be assured

Explanation: A Program Quality Assurance Plan outlines how program quality will be assured throughout the program's lifecycle.

182. Question: Which program management role is responsible for ensuring that program activities align with organizational strategy and goals?

A) Program Manager

B) Program Sponsor

C) Program Coordinator

D) Program Governance Board

Answer: B) Program Sponsor

Explanation: The Program Sponsor is responsible for ensuring that program activities align with organizational strategy and goals.

183. Question: In program management, what does the term "Program Roadmap" refer to?

A) A visual representation of program stakeholders

B) A tool for tracking program finances

C) A high-level plan outlining key program milestones and deliverables

D) A process for managing program dependencies

Answer: C) A high-level plan outlining key program milestones and deliverables

Explanation: A Program Roadmap is a high-level plan that outlines key program milestones and deliverables, providing a strategic view of the program.

184. Question: What is the primary purpose of a Program Issue Log?

A) To allocate resources to program activities

B) To document program benefits

C) To identify and track program issues and their resolution

D) To assess program risks

Answer: C) To identify and track program issues and their resolution

Explanation: A Program Issue Log is used to identify and track program issues and their resolution, ensuring they are addressed effectively.

185. Question: Which program management technique involves ranking program projects based on their strategic importance and alignment with organizational goals?

A) Program Evaluation and Review Technique (PERT)

B) Earned Value Management (EVM)

C) Program Prioritization

D) Critical Chain Method (CCM)

Answer: C) Program Prioritization

Explanation: Program Prioritization involves ranking program projects based on their strategic importance and alignment with organizational goals.

186. Question: What is the primary goal of program resource management?

A) To track program schedule performance

B) To allocate resources to program activities efficiently

C) To manage program finances

D) To ensure program compliance with regulations

Answer: B) To allocate resources to program activities efficiently

Explanation: Program resource management focuses on allocating resources to program activities efficiently to meet program objectives.

187. Question: Which program management framework emphasizes a holistic approach to managing business change through programs?

A) PRINCE2 (Projects IN Controlled Environments)

B) MSP (Managing Successful Programmes)

C) PMBOK (Project Management Body of Knowledge)

D) SAFe (Scaled Agile Framework)

Answer: B) MSP (Managing Successful Programmes)

Explanation: MSP emphasizes a holistic approach to managing business change through programs.

188. Question: In program management, what does the term "Program Risk Tolerance" refer to?

A) The willingness to accept program risks

B) The program's budget allocation

C) The timeline for program delivery

D) The program's stakeholder engagement strategy

Answer: A) The willingness to accept program risks

Explanation: Program Risk Tolerance refers to the organization's or program's willingness to accept and tolerate certain levels of risk.

189. Question: What is the primary purpose of a Program Closure Report?
A) To allocate resources to program activities
B) To assess the realization of program benefits against expected outcomes
C) To track program financial performance
D) To create a detailed program budget
Answer: B) To assess the realization of program benefits against expected outcomes

Explanation: A Program Closure Report assesses the realization of program benefits against expected outcomes, summarizing the program's achievements.

190. Question: Which program management approach emphasizes delivering value incrementally and frequently, with a focus on customer collaboration?
A) Agile Program Management
B) Traditional Program Management
C) Lean Program Management
D) Waterfall Program Management
Answer: A) Agile Program Management

Explanation: Agile Program Management focuses on delivering value incrementally and frequently, with a strong emphasis on customer collaboration and responding to change.

191. Question: What is the primary role of a Program Management Office (PMO) in program management?
A) To manage program finances
B) To provide administrative support to program managers
C) To oversee individual projects within the program
D) To support program managers and provide guidance and governance
Answer: D) To support program managers and provide guidance and governance

Explanation: The PMO's primary role in program management is to support program managers and provide guidance and governance to ensure program success.

192. Question: In program management, what does the term "Dependency Analysis" refer to?

A) A technique for estimating program durations

B) A process for identifying and managing program dependencies

C) A method for documenting program risks

D) A tool for tracking program financial performance

Answer: B) A process for identifying and managing program dependencies

Explanation: Dependency Analysis is a process used to identify and manage program dependencies, ensuring that activities are sequenced appropriately to achieve program goals.

193. Question: What is the primary goal of program stakeholder communication?

A) To allocate resources to program activities

B) To track program schedule performance

C) To provide relevant and timely information to program stakeholders

D) To manage program finances

Answer: C) To provide relevant and timely information to program stakeholders

Explanation: The primary goal of program stakeholder communication is to provide relevant and timely information to program stakeholders, ensuring they are well-informed and engaged in program activities.

194. Question: Which program management approach is best suited for highly uncertain and complex programs with evolving requirements?

A) Traditional Program Management

B) Waterfall Program Management

C) Adaptive Program Management

D) Lean Program Management

Answer: C) Adaptive Program Management

Explanation: Adaptive Program Management is well-suited for highly uncertain and complex programs with evolving requirements, as it allows for flexibility and adaptation.

195. Question: What is the primary purpose of a Program Issue Log?

A) To allocate resources to program activities

B) To visualize program benefits

C) To document and track program issues and their resolution

D) To assess program risks

Answer: C) To document and track program issues and their resolution

Explanation: A Program Issue Log is used to document and track program issues and their resolution, ensuring that they are addressed effectively.

196. Question: Which program management role is responsible for championing the program and advocating for its success?

A) Program Manager

B) Program Sponsor

C) Program Coordinator

D) Program Governance Board

Answer: B) Program Sponsor

Explanation: The Program Sponsor is responsible for championing the program and advocating for its success within the organization.

197. Question: In program management, what does the term "Program Risk Appetite" refer to?

A) The willingness to accept program risks

B) The program's budget allocation

C) The timeline for program delivery

D) The program's stakeholder engagement strategy

Answer: A) The willingness to accept program risks

Explanation: Program Risk Appetite refers to the organization's or program's willingness to accept and tolerate certain levels of risk.

198. Question: What is the primary purpose of a Program Closure Report?

A) To allocate resources to program activities

B) To assess the realization of program benefits against expected outcomes

C) To track program financial performance

D) To create a detailed program budget

Answer: B) To assess the realization of program benefits against expected outcomes

Explanation: A Program Closure Report assesses the realization of program benefits against expected outcomes, summarizing the program's achievements.

199. Question: In program management, what is the primary purpose of a Program Evaluation and Review Technique (PERT)?

A) To allocate resources to program activities

B) To visualize program benefits

C) To estimate program durations based on optimistic, pessimistic, and most likely scenarios

D) To track program financial performance

Answer: C) To estimate program durations based on optimistic, pessimistic, and most likely scenarios

Explanation: PERT is used in program management to estimate program durations based on optimistic, pessimistic, and most likely scenarios, helping with scheduling and planning.

200. Question: What is the primary focus of program stakeholder analysis?

A) To allocate resources to program activities

B) To track program schedule performance

C) To identify and understand the interests and influence of program stakeholders

D) To create a detailed program budget

Answer: C) To identify and understand the interests and influence of program stakeholders

Explanation: Program stakeholder analysis aims to identify and understand the interests and influence of program stakeholders, helping in effective stakeholder management.

201. Question: What is the primary purpose of a Program Benefits Realization Plan?

A) To allocate resources to program activities

B) To outline how program benefits will be achieved and measured

C) To visualize program stakeholders

D) To track program schedule performance

Answer: B) To outline how program benefits will be achieved and measured

Explanation: A Program Benefits Realization Plan outlines how program benefits will be achieved and measured throughout the program's lifecycle.

202. Question: Who is responsible for ensuring that program activities align with organizational strategy and goals?

A) Program Manager

B) Program Sponsor

C) Program Coordinator

D) Program Governance Board

Answer: B) Program Sponsor

Explanation: The Program Sponsor is responsible for ensuring that program activities align with organizational strategy and goals.

203. Question: In program management, what does the term "Program Roadmap" refer to?

A) A visual representation of program stakeholders

B) A tool for tracking program finances

C) A high-level plan outlining key program milestones and deliverables

D) A process for managing program dependencies

Answer: C) A high-level plan outlining key program milestones and deliverables

Explanation: A Program Roadmap is a high-level plan that outlines key program milestones and deliverables, providing a strategic view of the program.

204. Question: What is the primary purpose of a Program Issue Log?

A) To allocate resources to program activities

B) To document program benefits

C) To identify and track program issues and their resolution

D) To assess program risks

Answer: C) To identify and track program issues and their resolution

Explanation: A Program Issue Log is used to identify and track program issues and their resolution, ensuring they are addressed effectively.

205. Question: Which program management technique involves ranking program projects based on their strategic importance and alignment with organizational goals?

A) Program Evaluation and Review Technique (PERT)

B) Earned Value Management (EVM)

C) Program Prioritization

D) Critical Chain Method (CCM)

Answer: C) Program Prioritization

Explanation: Program Prioritization involves ranking program projects based on their strategic importance and alignment with organizational goals.

206. Question: What is the primary goal of program resource management?

A) To track program schedule performance

B) To allocate resources to program activities efficiently

C) To manage program finances

D) To ensure program compliance with regulations

Answer: B) To allocate resources to program activities efficiently

Explanation: Program resource management focuses on allocating resources to program activities efficiently to meet program objectives.

207. Question: Which program management framework emphasizes a holistic approach to managing business change through programs?

A) PRINCE2 (Projects IN Controlled Environments)

B) MSP (Managing Successful Programmes)

C) PMBOK (Project Management Body of Knowledge)

D) SAFe (Scaled Agile Framework)

Answer: B) MSP (Managing Successful Programmes)

Explanation: MSP emphasizes a holistic approach to managing business change through programs.

208. Question: In program management, what does the term "Program Risk Tolerance" refer to?

A) The willingness to accept program risks

B) The program's budget allocation

C) The timeline for program delivery

D) The program's stakeholder engagement strategy

Answer: A) The willingness to accept program risks

Explanation: Program Risk Tolerance refers to the organization's or program's willingness to accept and tolerate certain levels of risk.

209. Question: What is the primary purpose of a Program Closure Report?

A) To allocate resources to program activities

B) To assess the realization of program benefits against expected outcomes

C) To track program financial performance

D) To create a detailed program budget

Answer: B) To assess the realization of program benefits against expected outcomes

Explanation: A Program Closure Report assesses the realization of program benefits against expected outcomes, summarizing the program's achievements.

210. Question: Which program management approach emphasizes delivering value incrementally and frequently, with a focus on customer collaboration?

A) Agile Program Management

B) Traditional Program Management

C) Lean Program Management

D) Waterfall Program Management

Answer: A) Agile Program Management

Explanation: Agile Program Management focuses on delivering value incrementally and frequently, with a strong emphasis on customer collaboration and responding to change.

211. Question: What is the primary role of a Program Management Office (PMO) in program management?

A) To manage program finances

B) To provide administrative support to program managers

C) To oversee individual projects within the program

D) To support program managers and provide guidance and governance

Answer: D) To support program managers and provide guidance and governance

Explanation: The PMO's primary role in program management is to support program managers and provide guidance and governance to ensure program success.

212. Question: In program management, what does the term "Dependency Analysis" refer to?

A) A technique for estimating program durations

B) A process for identifying and managing program dependencies

C) A method for documenting program risks

D) A tool for tracking program financial performance

Answer: B) A process for identifying and managing program dependencies

Explanation: Dependency Analysis is a process used to identify and manage program dependencies, ensuring that activities are sequenced appropriately to achieve program goals.

213. Question: What is the primary goal of program stakeholder communication?

A) To allocate resources to program activities

B) To track program schedule performance

C) To provide relevant and timely information to program stakeholders

D) To manage program finances

Answer: C) To provide relevant and timely information to program stakeholders

Explanation: The primary goal of program stakeholder communication is to provide relevant and timely information to program stakeholders, ensuring they are well-informed and engaged in program activities.

214. Question: Which program management approach is best suited for highly uncertain and complex programs with evolving requirements?

A) Traditional Program Management

B) Waterfall Program Management

C) Adaptive Program Management

D) Lean Program Management

Answer: C) Adaptive Program Management

Explanation: Adaptive Program Management is well-suited for highly uncertain and complex programs with evolving requirements, as it allows for flexibility and adaptation.

215. Question: What is the primary purpose of a Program Issue Log?

A) To allocate resources to program activities

B) To visualize program benefits

C) To document and track program issues and their resolution

D) To assess program risks

Answer: C) To document and track program issues and their resolution

Explanation: A Program Issue Log is used to document and track program issues and their resolution, ensuring that they are addressed effectively.

216. Question: Which program management role is responsible for championing the program and advocating for its success?

A) Program Manager

B) Program Sponsor

C) Program Coordinator

D) Program Governance Board

Answer: B) Program Sponsor

Explanation: The Program Sponsor is responsible for championing the program and advocating for its success within the organization.

217. Question: In program management, what does the term "Program Risk Appetite" refer to?

A) The willingness to accept program risks

B) The program's budget allocation

C) The timeline for program delivery

D) The program's stakeholder engagement strategy

Answer: A) The willingness to accept program risks

Explanation: Program Risk Appetite refers to the organization's or program's willingness to accept and tolerate certain levels of risk.

218. Question: What is the primary purpose of a Program Closure Report?

A) To allocate resources to program activities

B) To assess the realization of program benefits against expected outcomes

C) To track program financial performance

D) To create a detailed program budget

Answer: B) To assess the realization of program benefits against expected outcomes

Explanation: A Program Closure Report assesses the realization of program benefits against expected outcomes, summarizing the program's achievements.

219. Question: In program management, what is the primary purpose of a Program Evaluation and Review Technique (PERT)?

A) To allocate resources to program activities

B) To visualize program benefits

C) To estimate program durations based on optimistic, pessimistic, and most likely scenarios

D) To track program financial performance

Answer: C) To estimate program durations based on optimistic, pessimistic, and most likely scenarios

Explanation: PERT is used in program management to estimate program durations based on optimistic, pessimistic, and most likely scenarios, helping with scheduling and planning.

220. Question: What is the primary focus of program stakeholder analysis?

A) To allocate resources to program activities

B) To track program schedule performance

C) To identify and understand the interests and influence of program stakeholders

D) To create a detailed program budget

Answer: C) To identify and understand the interests and influence of program stakeholders

Explanation: Program stakeholder analysis aims to identify and understand the interests and influence of program stakeholders, helping in effective stakeholder management.

221. Question: What is the primary purpose of a Program Benefits Realization Plan?

A) To allocate resources to program activities

B) To outline how program benefits will be achieved and measured

C) To visualize program stakeholders

D) To track program schedule performance

Answer: B) To outline how program benefits will be achieved and measured

Explanation: A Program Benefits Realization Plan outlines how program benefits will be achieved and measured throughout the program's lifecycle.

222. Question: Who is responsible for ensuring that program activities align with organizational strategy and goals?

A) Program Manager

B) Program Sponsor

C) Program Coordinator

D) Program Governance Board

Answer: B) Program Sponsor

Explanation: The Program Sponsor is responsible for ensuring that program activities align with organizational strategy and goals.

223. Question: In program management, what does the term "Program Roadmap" refer to?

A) A visual representation of program stakeholders

B) A tool for tracking program finances

C) A high-level plan outlining key program milestones and deliverables

D) A process for managing program dependencies

Answer: C) A high-level plan outlining key program milestones and deliverables

Explanation: A Program Roadmap is a high-level plan that outlines key program milestones and deliverables, providing a strategic view of the program.

224. Question: What is the primary purpose of a Program Issue Log?

A) To allocate resources to program activities

B) To document program benefits

C) To identify and track program issues and their resolution

D) To assess program risks

Answer: C) To identify and track program issues and their resolution

Explanation: A Program Issue Log is used to identify and track program issues and their resolution, ensuring they are addressed effectively.

225. Question: Which program management technique involves ranking program projects based on their strategic importance and alignment with organizational goals?

A) Program Evaluation and Review Technique (PERT)
B) Earned Value Management (EVM)
C) Program Prioritization
D) Critical Chain Method (CCM)

Answer: C) Program Prioritization

Explanation: Program Prioritization involves ranking program projects based on their strategic importance and alignment with organizational goals.

226. Question: What is the primary goal of program resource management?

A) To track program schedule performance
B) To allocate resources to program activities efficiently
C) To manage program finances
D) To ensure program compliance with regulations

Answer: B) To allocate resources to program activities efficiently

Explanation: Program resource management focuses on allocating resources to program activities efficiently to meet program objectives.

227. Question: Which program management framework emphasizes a holistic approach to managing business change through programs?

A) PRINCE2 (Projects IN Controlled Environments)
B) MSP (Managing Successful Programmes)
C) PMBOK (Project Management Body of Knowledge)
D) SAFe (Scaled Agile Framework)

Answer: B) MSP (Managing Successful Programmes)

Explanation: MSP emphasizes a holistic approach to managing business change through programs.

228. Question: In program management, what does the term "Program Risk Tolerance" refer to?

A) The willingness to accept program risks

B) The program's budget allocation

C) The timeline for program delivery

D) The program's stakeholder engagement strategy

Answer: A) The willingness to accept program risks

Explanation: Program Risk Tolerance refers to the organization's or program's willingness to accept and tolerate certain levels of risk.

229. Question: What is the primary purpose of a Program Closure Report?

A) To allocate resources to program activities

B) To assess the realization of program benefits against expected outcomes

C) To track program financial performance

D) To create a detailed program budget

Answer: B) To assess the realization of program benefits against expected outcomes

Explanation: A Program Closure Report assesses the realization of program benefits against expected outcomes, summarizing the program's achievements.

230. Question: Which program management approach emphasizes delivering value incrementally and frequently, with a focus on customer collaboration?

A) Agile Program Management

B) Traditional Program Management

C) Lean Program Management

D) Waterfall Program Management

Answer: A) Agile Program Management

Explanation: Agile Program Management focuses on delivering value incrementally and frequently, with a strong emphasis on customer collaboration and responding to change.

231. Question: What is the primary role of a Program Management Office (PMO) in program management?

A) To manage program finances

B) To provide administrative support to program managers

C) To oversee individual projects within the program

D) To support program managers and provide guidance and governance

Answer: D) To support program managers and provide guidance and governance

Explanation: The PMO's primary role in program management is to support program managers and provide guidance and governance to ensure program success.

232. Question: In program management, what does the term "Dependency Analysis" refer to?

A) A technique for estimating program durations

B) A process for identifying and managing program dependencies

C) A method for documenting program risks

D) A tool for tracking program financial performance

Answer: B) A process for identifying and managing program dependencies

Explanation: Dependency Analysis is a process used to identify and manage program dependencies, ensuring that activities are sequenced appropriately to achieve program goals.

233. Question: What is the primary goal of program stakeholder communication?

A) To allocate resources to program activities

B) To track program schedule performance

C) To provide relevant and timely information to program stakeholders

D) To manage program finances

Answer: C) To provide relevant and timely information to program stakeholders

Explanation: The primary goal of program stakeholder communication is to provide relevant and timely information to program stakeholders, ensuring they are well-informed and engaged in program activities.

234. Question: Which program management approach is best suited for highly uncertain and complex programs with evolving requirements?

A) Traditional Program Management

B) Waterfall Program Management

C) Adaptive Program Management

D) Lean Program Management

Answer: C) Adaptive Program Management

Explanation: Adaptive Program Management is well-suited for highly uncertain and complex programs with evolving requirements, as it allows for flexibility and adaptation.

235. Question: What is the primary purpose of a Program Issue Log?

A) To allocate resources to program activities

B) To visualize program benefits

C) To document and track program issues and their resolution

D) To assess program risks

Answer: C) To document and track program issues and their resolution

Explanation: A Program Issue Log is used to document and track program issues and their resolution, ensuring that they are addressed effectively.

236. Question: Which program management role is responsible for championing the program and advocating for its success?

A) Program Manager

B) Program Sponsor

C) Program Coordinator

D) Program Governance Board

Answer: B) Program Sponsor

Explanation: The Program Sponsor is responsible for championing the program and advocating for its success within the organization.

237. Question: In program management, what does the term "Program Risk Appetite" refer to?

A) The willingness to accept program risks

B) The program's budget allocation

C) The timeline for program delivery

D) The program's stakeholder engagement strategy

Answer: A) The willingness to accept program risks

Explanation: Program Risk Appetite refers to the organization's or program's willingness to accept and tolerate certain levels of risk.

238. Question: What is the primary purpose of a Program Closure Report?

A) To allocate resources to program activities

B) To assess the realization of program benefits against expected outcomes

C) To track program financial performance

D) To create a detailed program budget

Answer: B) To assess the realization of program benefits against expected outcomes

Explanation: A Program Closure Report assesses the realization of program benefits against expected outcomes, summarizing the program's achievements.

239. Question: In program management, what is the primary purpose of a Program Evaluation and Review Technique (PERT)?

A) To allocate resources to program activities

B) To visualize program benefits

C) To estimate program durations based on optimistic, pessimistic, and most likely scenarios

D) To track program financial performance

Answer: C) To estimate program durations based on optimistic, pessimistic, and most likely scenarios

Explanation: PERT is used in program management to estimate program durations based on optimistic, pessimistic, and most likely scenarios, helping with scheduling and planning.

240. Question: What is the primary focus of program stakeholder analysis?

A) To allocate resources to program activities

B) To track program schedule performance

C) To identify and understand the interests and influence of program stakeholders

D) To create a detailed program budget

Answer: C) To identify and understand the interests and influence of program stakeholders

Explanation: Program stakeholder analysis aims to identify and understand the interests and influence of program stakeholders, helping in effective stakeholder management.

241. Question: What is the primary purpose of a Program Benefits Realization Plan?

A) To allocate resources to program activities

B) To outline how program benefits will be achieved and measured

C) To visualize program stakeholders

D) To track program schedule performance

Answer: B) To outline how program benefits will be achieved and measured

Explanation: A Program Benefits Realization Plan outlines how program benefits will be achieved and measured throughout the program's lifecycle.

242. Question: Who is responsible for ensuring that program activities align with organizational strategy and goals?

A) Program Manager

B) Program Sponsor

C) Program Coordinator

D) Program Governance Board

Answer: B) Program Sponsor

Explanation: The Program Sponsor is responsible for ensuring that program activities align with organizational strategy and goals.

243. Question: In program management, what does the term "Program Roadmap" refer to?

A) A visual representation of program stakeholders

B) A tool for tracking program finances

C) A high-level plan outlining key program milestones and deliverables

D) A process for managing program dependencies

Answer: C) A high-level plan outlining key program milestones and deliverables

Explanation: A Program Roadmap is a high-level plan that outlines key program milestones and deliverables, providing a strategic view of the program.

244. Question: What is the primary purpose of a Program Issue Log?

A) To allocate resources to program activities

B) To document program benefits

C) To identify and track program issues and their resolution

D) To assess program risks

Answer: C) To identify and track program issues and their resolution

Explanation: A Program Issue Log is used to identify and track program issues and their resolution, ensuring they are addressed effectively.

245. Question: Which program management technique involves ranking program projects based on their strategic importance and alignment with organizational goals?

A) Program Evaluation and Review Technique (PERT)

B) Earned Value Management (EVM)

C) Program Prioritization

D) Critical Chain Method (CCM)

Answer: C) Program Prioritization

Explanation: Program Prioritization involves ranking program projects based on their strategic importance and alignment with organizational goals.

246. Question: What is the primary goal of program resource management?

A) To track program schedule performance

B) To allocate resources to program activities efficiently

C) To manage program finances

D) To ensure program compliance with regulations

Answer: B) To allocate resources to program activities efficiently

Explanation: Program resource management focuses on allocating resources to program activities efficiently to meet program objectives.

247. Question: Which program management framework emphasizes a holistic approach to managing business change through programs?

A) PRINCE2 (Projects IN Controlled Environments)

B) MSP (Managing Successful Programmes)

C) PMBOK (Project Management Body of Knowledge)

D) SAFe (Scaled Agile Framework)

Answer: B) MSP (Managing Successful Programmes)

Explanation: MSP emphasizes a holistic approach to managing business change through programs.

248. Question: In program management, what does the term "Program Risk Tolerance" refer to?

A) The willingness to accept program risks

B) The program's budget allocation

C) The timeline for program delivery

D) The program's stakeholder engagement strategy

Answer: A) The willingness to accept program risks

Explanation: Program Risk Tolerance refers to the organization's or program's willingness to accept and tolerate certain levels of risk.

249. Question: What is the primary purpose of a Program Closure Report?

A) To allocate resources to program activities

B) To assess the realization of program benefits against expected outcomes

C) To track program financial performance

D) To create a detailed program budget

Answer: B) To assess the realization of program benefits against expected outcomes

Explanation: A Program Closure Report assesses the realization of program benefits against expected outcomes, summarizing the program's achievements.

250. Question: Which program management approach emphasizes delivering value incrementally and frequently, with a focus on customer collaboration?

A) Agile Program Management

B) Traditional Program Management

C) Lean Program Management

D) Waterfall Program Management

Answer: A) Agile Program Management

Explanation: Agile Program Management focuses on delivering value incrementally and frequently, with a strong emphasis on customer collaboration and responding to change.

251. Question: What is the primary role of a Program Management Office (PMO) in program management?

A) To manage program finances

B) To provide administrative support to program managers

C) To oversee individual projects within the program

D) To support program managers and provide guidance and governance

Answer: D) To support program managers and provide guidance and governance

Explanation: The PMO's primary role in program management is to support program managers and provide guidance and governance to ensure program success.

252. Question: In program management, what does the term "Dependency Analysis" refer to?

A) A technique for estimating program durations

B) A process for identifying and managing program dependencies

C) A method for documenting program risks

D) A tool for tracking program financial performance

Answer: B) A process for identifying and managing program dependencies

Explanation: Dependency Analysis is a process used to identify and manage program dependencies, ensuring that activities are sequenced appropriately to achieve program goals.

253. Question: What is the primary goal of program stakeholder communication?

A) To allocate resources to program activities

B) To track program schedule performance

C) To provide relevant and timely information to program stakeholders

D) To manage program finances

Answer: C) To provide relevant and timely information to program stakeholders

Explanation: The primary goal of program stakeholder communication is to provide relevant and timely information to program stakeholders, ensuring they are well-informed and engaged in program activities.

254. Question: Which program management approach is best suited for highly uncertain and complex programs with evolving requirements?

A) Traditional Program Management

B) Waterfall Program Management

C) Adaptive Program Management

D) Lean Program Management

Answer: C) Adaptive Program Management

Explanation: Adaptive Program Management is well-suited for highly uncertain and complex programs with evolving requirements, as it allows for flexibility and adaptation.

255. Question: What is the primary purpose of a Program Issue Log?

A) To allocate resources to program activities

B) To visualize program benefits

C) To document and track program issues and their resolution

D) To assess program risks

Answer: C) To document and track program issues and their resolution

Explanation: A Program Issue Log is used to document and track program issues and their resolution, ensuring that they are addressed effectively.

256. Question: Which program management role is responsible for championing the program and advocating for its success?

A) Program Manager

B) Program Sponsor

C) Program Coordinator

D) Program Governance Board

Answer: B) Program Sponsor

Explanation: The Program Sponsor is responsible for championing the program and advocating for its success within the organization.

257. Question: In program management, what does the term "Program Risk Appetite" refer to?

A) The willingness to accept program risks

B) The program's budget allocation

C) The timeline for program delivery

D) The program's stakeholder engagement strategy

Answer: A) The willingness to accept program risks

Explanation: Program Risk Appetite refers to the organization's or program's willingness to accept and tolerate certain levels of risk.

258. Question: What is the primary purpose of a Program Closure Report?

A) To allocate resources to program activities

B) To assess the realization of program benefits against expected outcomes

C) To track program financial performance

D) To create a detailed program budget

Answer: B) To assess the realization of program benefits against expected outcomes

Explanation: A Program Closure Report assesses the realization of program benefits against expected outcomes, summarizing the program's achievements.

259. Question: In program management, what is the primary purpose of a Program Evaluation and Review Technique (PERT)?

A) To allocate resources to program activities

B) To visualize program benefits

C) To estimate program durations based on optimistic, pessimistic, and most likely scenarios

D) To track program financial performance

Answer: C) To estimate program durations based on optimistic, pessimistic, and most likely scenarios

Explanation: PERT is used in program management to estimate program durations based on optimistic, pessimistic, and most likely scenarios, helping with scheduling and planning.

260. Question: What is the primary focus of program stakeholder analysis?

A) To allocate resources to program activities

B) To track program schedule performance

C) To identify and understand the interests and influence of program stakeholders

D) To create a detailed program budget

Answer: C) To identify and understand the interests and influence of program stakeholders

Explanation: Program stakeholder analysis aims to identify and understand the interests and influence of program stakeholders, helping in effective stakeholder management.

261. Question: In program management, what is the primary purpose of a Program Governance Board?

A) To allocate resources to program activities

B) To provide administrative support to program managers

C) To oversee individual projects within the program

D) To provide guidance and governance to the program

Answer: D) To provide guidance and governance to the program

Explanation: A Program Governance Board's primary role is to provide guidance and governance to the program, ensuring alignment with organizational objectives.

262. Question: Which program management approach focuses on maximizing value delivery while minimizing waste and unnecessary work?

A) Agile Program Management

B) Traditional Program Management

C) Lean Program Management

D) Waterfall Program Management

Answer: C) Lean Program Management

Explanation: Lean Program Management emphasizes maximizing value delivery while minimizing waste and unnecessary work.

263. Question: What is the primary goal of program stakeholder engagement?

A) To allocate resources to program activities

B) To track program schedule performance

C) To build positive relationships and foster collaboration with program stakeholders

D) To create a detailed program budget

Answer: C) To build positive relationships and foster collaboration with program stakeholders

Explanation: The primary goal of program stakeholder engagement is to build positive relationships and foster collaboration with program stakeholders, promoting their active involvement in the program.

264. Question: Which program management role is responsible for day-to-day program execution and ensuring that program objectives are met?

A) Program Manager

B) Program Sponsor

C) Program Coordinator

D) Program Governance Board

Answer: A) Program Manager

Explanation: The Program Manager is responsible for day-to-day program execution and ensuring that program objectives are met.

265. Question: What is the primary purpose of a Program Risk Register?

A) To allocate resources to program activities

B) To visualize program benefits

C) To document and track program risks and their mitigation strategies

D) To assess program financial performance

Answer: C) To document and track program risks and their mitigation strategies

Explanation: A Program Risk Register is used to document and track program risks and their mitigation strategies, helping the program proactively manage potential issues.

266. Question: Which program management framework provides a set of principles, processes, and roles for scaling agile practices to large programs and portfolios?

A) PRINCE2 (Projects IN Controlled Environments)

B) MSP (Managing Successful Programmes)

C) PMBOK (Project Management Body of Knowledge)

D) SAFe (Scaled Agile Framework)

Answer: D) SAFe (Scaled Agile Framework)

Explanation: SAFe is a framework that provides principles, processes, and roles for scaling agile practices to large programs and portfolios.

267. Question: What is the primary purpose of a Program Financial Report?

A) To allocate resources to program activities

B) To assess the realization of program benefits against expected outcomes

C) To track program financial performance and expenditures

D) To create a detailed program schedule

Answer: C) To track program financial performance and expenditures

Explanation: A Program Financial Report is used to track program financial performance and expenditures, ensuring that the program stays within budget.

268. Question: In program management, what does the term "Program Portfolio" refer to?

A) A collection of individual projects within a program

B) A visual representation of program stakeholders

C) A document outlining program benefits

D) A strategic collection of related programs and projects managed as a group

Answer: D) A strategic collection of related programs and projects managed as a group

Explanation: A Program Portfolio refers to a strategic collection of related programs and projects managed as a group to achieve overarching organizational objectives.

269. Question: What is the primary focus of program quality management?

A) To allocate resources to program activities

B) To track program schedule performance

C) To ensure that program deliverables meet specified quality standards

D) To create a detailed program budget

Answer: C) To ensure that program deliverables meet specified quality standards

Explanation: Program quality management focuses on ensuring that program deliverables meet specified quality standards and that quality is maintained throughout the program.

270. Question: Which program management role is responsible for securing funding and resources for the program?

A) Program Manager

B) Program Sponsor

C) Program Coordinator

D) Program Governance Board

Answer: B) Program Sponsor

Explanation: The Program Sponsor is responsible for securing funding and resources for the program and ensuring it aligns with organizational goals.

271. Question: What is the primary purpose of a Program Stakeholder Engagement Plan?

A) To allocate resources to program activities

B) To track program schedule performance

C) To document the strategy for engaging and managing program stakeholders

D) To create a detailed program budget

Answer: C) To document the strategy for engaging and managing program stakeholders

Explanation: A Program Stakeholder Engagement Plan is used to document the strategy for engaging and managing program stakeholders effectively.

272. Question: In program management, what does the term "Program Risk Appetite" refer to?

A) The willingness to accept program risks

B) The program's budget allocation

C) The timeline for program delivery

D) The program's stakeholder engagement strategy

Answer: A) The willingness to accept program risks

Explanation: Program Risk Appetite refers to the organization's or program's willingness to accept and tolerate certain levels of risk.

273. Question: What is the primary purpose of a Program Closure Report?

A) To allocate resources to program activities

B) To assess the realization of program benefits against expected outcomes

C) To track program financial performance

D) To create a detailed program budget

Answer: B) To assess the realization of program benefits against expected outcomes

Explanation: A Program Closure Report assesses the realization of program benefits against expected outcomes, summarizing the program's achievements.

274. Question: In program management, what is the primary purpose of a Program Evaluation and Review Technique (PERT)?

A) To allocate resources to program activities

B) To visualize program benefits

C) To estimate program durations based on optimistic, pessimistic, and most likely scenarios

D) To track program financial performance

Answer: C) To estimate program durations based on optimistic, pessimistic, and most likely scenarios

Explanation: PERT is used in program management to estimate program durations based on optimistic, pessimistic, and most likely scenarios, helping with scheduling and planning.

275. Question: What is the primary focus of program stakeholder analysis?

A) To allocate resources to program activities

B) To track program schedule performance

C) To identify and understand the interests and influence of program stakeholders

D) To create a detailed program budget

Answer: C) To identify and understand the interests and influence of program stakeholders

Explanation: Program stakeholder analysis aims to identify and understand the interests and influence of program stakeholders, helping in effective stakeholder management.

276. Question: What is the primary purpose of a Program Governance Plan?

A) To allocate resources to program activities

B) To track program schedule performance

C) To document the program's governance structure and decision-making processes

D) To create a detailed program budget

Answer: C) To document the program's governance structure and decision-making processes

Explanation: A Program Governance Plan is used to document the program's governance structure and decision-making processes, ensuring clarity and transparency.

277. Question: In program management, what does the term "Program Risk Tolerance" refer to?

A) The willingness to accept program risks

B) The program's budget allocation

C) The timeline for program delivery

D) The program's stakeholder engagement strategy

Answer: A) The willingness to accept program risks

Explanation: Program Risk Tolerance refers to the organization's or program's willingness to accept and tolerate certain levels of risk.

278. Question: What is the primary goal of program stakeholder communication?

A) To allocate resources to program activities

B) To track program schedule performance

C) To provide relevant and timely information to program stakeholders

D) To manage program finances

Answer: C) To provide relevant and timely information to program stakeholders

Explanation: The primary goal of program stakeholder communication is to provide relevant and timely information to program stakeholders, ensuring they are well-informed and engaged in program activities.

279. Question: Which program management approach is best suited for highly uncertain and complex programs with evolving requirements?

A) Traditional Program Management

B) Waterfall Program Management

C) Adaptive Program Management

D) Lean Program Management

Answer: C) Adaptive Program Management

Explanation: Adaptive Program Management is well-suited for highly uncertain and complex programs with evolving requirements, as it allows for flexibility and adaptation.

280. Question: What is the primary purpose of a Program Benefits Realization Plan?

A) To allocate resources to program activities

B) To outline how program benefits will be achieved and measured

C) To visualize program stakeholders

D) To track program schedule performance

Answer: B) To outline how program benefits will be achieved and measured

Explanation: A Program Benefits Realization Plan outlines how program benefits will be achieved and measured throughout the program's lifecycle.

281. Question: What is the primary purpose of a Program Charter in program management?

A) To allocate resources to program activities

B) To assess program benefits realization

C) To outline the program's objectives, scope, and stakeholders

D) To track program financial performance

Answer: C) To outline the program's objectives, scope, and stakeholders

Explanation: A Program Charter outlines the program's objectives, scope, and stakeholders, providing a clear understanding of the program's purpose and boundaries.

282. Question: Which program management role is responsible for resolving conflicts and issues within the program team?

A) Program Manager

B) Program Sponsor

C) Program Coordinator

D) Program Governance Board

Answer: A) Program Manager

Explanation: The Program Manager is responsible for resolving conflicts and issues within the program team to ensure smooth execution.

283. Question: What is the primary purpose of a Program Benefits Register?

A) To allocate resources to program activities

B) To visualize program stakeholders

C) To document and track program benefits, their owners, and their realization status

D) To assess program schedule performance

Answer: C) To document and track program benefits, their owners, and their realization status

Explanation: A Program Benefits Register is used to document and track program benefits, their owners, and their realization status throughout the program.

284. Question: In program management, what does the term "Program Governance" refer to?

A) The program's budget allocation

B) The program's schedule performance

C) The framework of policies, procedures, and decision-making structures that guide program execution

D) The program's stakeholder engagement strategy

Answer: C) The framework of policies, procedures, and decision-making structures that guide program execution

Explanation: Program Governance refers to the framework of policies, procedures, and decision-making structures that guide program execution and oversight.

285. Question: What is the primary focus of program stakeholder communication?

A) To allocate resources to program activities

B) To track program schedule performance

C) To provide relevant and timely information to program stakeholders

D) To manage program finances

Answer: C) To provide relevant and timely information to program stakeholders

Explanation: The primary goal of program stakeholder communication is to provide relevant and timely information to program stakeholders, ensuring they are well-informed and engaged in program activities.

286. Question: Which program management approach emphasizes delivering value incrementally and frequently, with a focus on customer collaboration?

A) Agile Program Management

B) Traditional Program Management

C) Lean Program Management

D) Waterfall Program Management

Answer: A) Agile Program Management

Explanation: Agile Program Management focuses on delivering value incrementally and frequently, with a strong emphasis on customer collaboration and responding to change.

287. Question: What is the primary goal of program resource management?

A) To track program schedule performance

B) To allocate resources to program activities efficiently

C) To manage program finances

D) To ensure program compliance with regulations

Answer: B) To allocate resources to program activities efficiently

Explanation: Program resource management focuses on allocating resources to program activities efficiently to meet program objectives.

288. Question: In program management, what does the term "Program Portfolio" refer to?

A) A collection of individual projects within a program

B) A visual representation of program stakeholders

C) A document outlining program benefits

D) A strategic collection of related programs and projects managed as a group

Answer: D) A strategic collection of related programs and projects managed as a group

Explanation: A Program Portfolio refers to a strategic collection of related programs and projects managed as a group to achieve overarching organizational objectives.

289. Question: What is the primary purpose of a Program Quality Management Plan?

A) To allocate resources to program activities

B) To track program schedule performance

C) To define how program quality will be planned, assured, and controlled

D) To create a detailed program budget

Answer: C) To define how program quality will be planned, assured, and controlled

Explanation: A Program Quality Management Plan defines how program quality will be planned, assured, and controlled to meet specified standards.

290. Question: Which program management role is responsible for securing funding and resources for the program?

A) Program Manager

B) Program Sponsor

C) Program Coordinator

D) Program Governance Board

Answer: B) Program Sponsor

Explanation: The Program Sponsor is responsible for securing funding and resources for the program and ensuring it aligns with organizational goals.

291. Question: What is the primary purpose of a Program Stakeholder Engagement Plan?

A) To allocate resources to program activities

B) To track program schedule performance

C) To document the strategy for engaging and managing program stakeholders

D) To create a detailed program budget

Answer: C) To document the strategy for engaging and managing program stakeholders

Explanation: A Program Stakeholder Engagement Plan is used to document the strategy for engaging and managing program stakeholders effectively.

292. Question: In program management, what does the term "Program Risk Tolerance" refer to?

A) The willingness to accept program risks

B) The program's budget allocation

C) The timeline for program delivery

D) The program's stakeholder engagement strategy

Answer: A) The willingness to accept program risks

Explanation: Program Risk Tolerance refers to the organization's or program's willingness to accept and tolerate certain levels of risk.

293. Question: What is the primary purpose of a Program Closure Report?

A) To allocate resources to program activities

B) To assess the realization of program benefits against expected outcomes

C) To track program financial performance

D) To create a detailed program budget

Answer: B) To assess the realization of program benefits against expected outcomes

Explanation: A Program Closure Report assesses the realization of program benefits against expected outcomes, summarizing the program's achievements.

294. Question: In program management, what does the term "Program Evaluation and Review Technique (PERT)" refer to?

A) A tool for tracking program finances

B) A process for identifying and managing program dependencies

C) A method for documenting program risks

D) A technique for estimating program durations based on optimistic, pessimistic, and most likely scenarios

Answer: D) A technique for estimating program durations based on optimistic, pessimistic, and most likely scenarios

Explanation: PERT is a technique used in program management to estimate program durations based on optimistic, pessimistic, and most likely scenarios, aiding in scheduling and planning.

295. Question: What is the primary focus of program stakeholder analysis?

A) To allocate resources to program activities

B) To track program schedule performance

C) To identify and understand the interests and influence of program stakeholders

D) To create a detailed program budget

Answer: C) To identify and understand the interests and influence of program stakeholders

Explanation: Program stakeholder analysis focuses on identifying and understanding the interests and influence of program stakeholders, facilitating effective stakeholder management.

296. Question: What is the primary purpose of a Program Governance Plan?

A) To allocate resources to program activities

B) To track program schedule performance

C) To document the program's governance structure and decision-making processes

D) To create a detailed program budget

Answer: C) To document the program's governance structure and decision-making processes

Explanation: A Program Governance Plan is used to document the program's governance structure and decision-making processes, ensuring clarity and transparency.

297. Question: In program management, what does the term "Program Risk Appetite" refer to?

A) The willingness to accept program risks

B) The program's budget allocation

C) The timeline for program delivery

D) The program's stakeholder engagement strategy

Answer: A) The willingness to accept program risks

Explanation: Program Risk Appetite refers to the organization's or program's willingness to accept and tolerate certain levels of risk.

298. Question: What is the primary goal of program stakeholder communication?

A) To allocate resources to program activities

B) To track program schedule performance

C) To provide relevant and timely information to program stakeholders

D) To manage program finances

Answer: C) To provide relevant and timely information to program stakeholders

Explanation: The primary goal of program stakeholder communication is to provide relevant and timely information to program stakeholders, ensuring they are well-informed and engaged in program activities.

299. Question: Which program management approach is best suited for highly uncertain and complex programs with evolving requirements?

A) Traditional Program Management

B) Waterfall Program Management

C) Adaptive Program Management

D) Lean Program Management

Answer: C) Adaptive Program Management

Explanation: Adaptive Program Management is well-suited for highly uncertain and complex programs with evolving requirements, as it allows for flexibility and adaptation.

300. Question: What is the primary purpose of a Program Benefits Realization Plan?

A) To allocate resources to program activities

B) To outline how program benefits will be achieved and measured

C) To visualize program stakeholders

D) To track program schedule performance

Answer: B) To outline how program benefits will be achieved and measured

Explanation: A Program Benefits Realization Plan outlines how program benefits will be achieved and measured throughout the program's lifecycle.

301. Question: What is the primary purpose of a Program Benefits Realization Review?

A) To allocate resources to program activities

B) To assess program risks

C) To evaluate the achievement of program benefits against expectations

D) To track program financial performance

Answer: C) To evaluate the achievement of program benefits against expectations

Explanation: A Program Benefits Realization Review assesses the actual achievement of program benefits against the expectations defined in the program's objectives.

302. Question: Which program management role is responsible for ensuring that program activities are compliant with relevant laws and regulations?

A) Program Manager

B) Program Sponsor

C) Program Compliance Officer

D) Program Governance Board

Answer: C) Program Compliance Officer

Explanation: The Program Compliance Officer is responsible for ensuring that program activities adhere to relevant laws and regulations.

303. Question: In program management, what is the primary purpose of a Program Risk Mitigation Plan?

A) To allocate resources to program activities

B) To document and track program risks and their mitigation strategies

C) To assess program financial performance

D) To create a detailed program budget

Answer: B) To document and track program risks and their mitigation strategies

Explanation: A Program Risk Mitigation Plan is used to document and track program risks and their mitigation strategies to reduce potential negative impacts.

304. Question: What is the primary focus of program stakeholder engagement?

A) To allocate resources to program activities

B) To assess program benefits realization

C) To build positive relationships and foster collaboration with program stakeholders

D) To track program schedule performance

Answer: C) To build positive relationships and foster collaboration with program stakeholders

Explanation: The primary focus of program stakeholder engagement is to build positive relationships and foster collaboration with program stakeholders, promoting their active involvement in the program.

305. Question: Which program management framework emphasizes the importance of strategic alignment, benefits realization, and governance?

A) Agile Program Management

B) MSP (Managing Successful Programmes)

C) Lean Program Management

D) PRINCE2 (Projects IN Controlled Environments)

Answer: B) MSP (Managing Successful Programmes)

Explanation: MSP (Managing Successful Programmes) is a framework that emphasizes strategic alignment, benefits realization, and governance in program management.

306. Question: What is the primary goal of program resource allocation?

A) To assess program risks

B) To allocate resources to program activities optimally

C) To manage program finances

D) To create a detailed program schedule

Answer: B) To allocate resources to program activities optimally

Explanation: The primary goal of program resource allocation is to allocate resources to program activities optimally, ensuring efficient resource utilization.

307. Question: In program management, what does the term "Program KPI" stand for?

A) Key Program Initiatives

B) Key Performance Indicators

C) Key Program Investments

D) Key Program Influences

Answer: B) Key Performance Indicators

Explanation: Program KPI stands for Key Performance Indicators, which are metrics used to measure program performance and progress.

308. Question: What is the primary purpose of a Program Communication Plan?

A) To allocate resources to program activities

B) To track program schedule performance

C) To outline how program communication will be managed and executed

D) To create a detailed program budget

Answer: C) To outline how program communication will be managed and executed

Explanation: A Program Communication Plan outlines how program communication will be managed and executed, ensuring effective stakeholder communication.

309. Question: Which program management approach is best suited for projects with well-defined requirements and minimal uncertainty?

A) Traditional Program Management

B) Waterfall Program Management

C) Adaptive Program Management

D) Lean Program Management

Answer: A) Traditional Program Management

Explanation: Traditional Program Management, including the Waterfall approach, is best suited for projects with well-defined requirements and minimal uncertainty.

310. Question: What is the primary purpose of a Program Stakeholder Register?

A) To allocate resources to program activities

B) To visualize program benefits

C) To document and categorize program stakeholders and their interests

D) To assess program schedule performance

Answer: C) To document and categorize program stakeholders and their interests

Explanation: A Program Stakeholder Register is used to document and categorize program stakeholders and their interests, aiding in stakeholder management.

311. Question: What is the primary purpose of a Program Governance Board?

A) To allocate resources to program activities

B) To provide administrative support to program managers

C) To oversee individual projects within the program

D) To provide guidance and governance to the program

Answer: D) To provide guidance and governance to the program

Explanation: A Program Governance Board's primary role is to provide guidance and governance to the program, ensuring alignment with organizational objectives.

312. Question: In program management, what does the term "Program Roadmap" refer to?

A) A visual representation of program stakeholders

B) A document outlining program benefits

C) A high-level plan that outlines program milestones and key activities

D) A tool for tracking program finances

Answer: C) A high-level plan that outlines program milestones and key activities

Explanation: A Program Roadmap is a high-level plan that outlines program milestones and key activities, providing a strategic overview of the program.

313. Question: What is the primary focus of program quality assurance?

A) To allocate resources to program activities

B) To assess program benefits realization

C) To ensure that program processes and activities conform to established standards

D) To track program financial performance

Answer: C) To ensure that program processes and activities conform to established standards

Explanation: Program quality assurance focuses on ensuring that program processes and activities conform to established standards, promoting quality throughout the program.

314. Question: What is the primary purpose of a Program Budget Report?

A) To allocate resources to program activities

B) To assess the realization of program benefits against expected outcomes

C) To track program financial performance against the approved budget

D) To create a detailed program schedule

Answer: C) To track program financial performance against the approved budget

Explanation: A Program Budget Report is used to track program financial performance against the approved budget, helping to manage expenditures.

315. Question: Which program management role is responsible for day-to-day program execution and ensuring that program objectives are met?

A) Program Manager

B) Program Sponsor

C) Program Coordinator

D) Program Governance Board

Answer: A) Program Manager

Explanation: The Program Manager is responsible for day-to-day program execution and ensuring that program objectives are met.

316. Question: In program management, what is the primary purpose of a Program Risk Register?

A) To allocate resources to program activities

B) To visualize program benefits

C) To document and track program risks and their mitigation strategies

D) To assess program financial performance

Answer: C) To document and track program risks and their mitigation strategies

Explanation: A Program Risk Register is used to document and track program risks and their mitigation strategies, helping the program proactively manage potential issues.

317. Question: What is the primary goal of program stakeholder engagement?

A) To allocate resources to program activities

B) To track program schedule performance

C) To build positive relationships and foster collaboration with program stakeholders

D) To create a detailed program budget

Answer: C) To build positive relationships and foster collaboration with program stakeholders

Explanation: The primary goal of program stakeholder engagement is to build positive relationships and foster collaboration with program stakeholders, promoting their active involvement in the program.

318. Question: What is the primary purpose of a Program Closure Report?

A) To allocate resources to program activities

B) To assess the realization of program benefits against expected outcomes

C) To track program financial performance

D) To create a detailed program budget

Answer: B) To assess the realization of program benefits against expected outcomes

Explanation: A Program Closure Report assesses the realization of program benefits against expected outcomes, summarizing the program's achievements.

319. Question: In program management, what does the term "Program Evaluation and Review Technique (PERT)" refer to?

A) A tool for tracking program finances

B) A process for identifying and managing program dependencies

C) A method for documenting program risks

D) A technique for estimating program durations based on optimistic, pessimistic, and most likely scenarios

Answer: D) A technique for estimating program durations based on optimistic, pessimistic, and most likely scenarios

Explanation: PERT is a technique used in program management to estimate program durations based on optimistic, pessimistic, and most likely scenarios, aiding in scheduling and planning.

320. Question: What is the primary focus of program stakeholder analysis?

A) To allocate resources to program activities

B) To track program schedule performance

C) To identify and understand the interests and influence of program stakeholders

D) To create a detailed program budget

Answer: C) To identify and understand the interests and influence of program stakeholders

Explanation: Program stakeholder analysis focuses on identifying and understanding the interests and influence of program stakeholders, facilitating effective stakeholder management.

321. Question: What is the primary purpose of a Program Benefits Realization Plan?

A) To allocate resources to program activities

B) To assess program risks

C) To outline how program benefits will be achieved and measured

D) To create a detailed program schedule

Answer: C) To outline how program benefits will be achieved and measured

Explanation: A Program Benefits Realization Plan outlines how program benefits will be achieved and measured throughout the program's lifecycle.

322. Question: Which program management role is responsible for resolving conflicts and issues within the program team?

A) Program Manager

B) Program Sponsor

C) Program Coordinator

D) Program Governance Board

Answer: A) Program Manager

Explanation: The Program Manager is responsible for resolving conflicts and issues within the program team to ensure smooth execution.

323. Question: In program management, what does the term "Program Governance" refer to?

A) The program's budget allocation

B) The program's schedule performance

C) The framework of policies, procedures, and decision-making structures that guide program execution

D) The program's stakeholder engagement strategy

Answer: C) The framework of policies, procedures, and decision-making structures that guide program execution

Explanation: Program Governance refers to the framework of policies, procedures, and decision-making structures that guide program execution and oversight.

324. Question: What is the primary focus of program stakeholder communication?

A) To allocate resources to program activities

B) To assess program benefits realization

C) To provide relevant and timely information to program stakeholders

D) To manage program finances

Answer: C) To provide relevant and timely information to program stakeholders

Explanation: The primary goal of program stakeholder communication is to provide relevant and timely information to program stakeholders, ensuring they are well-informed and engaged in program activities.

325. Question: Which program management approach emphasizes delivering value incrementally and frequently, with a focus on customer collaboration?

A) Agile Program Management

B) Traditional Program Management

C) Lean Program Management

D) Waterfall Program Management

Answer: A) Agile Program Management

Explanation: Agile Program Management focuses on delivering value incrementally and frequently, with a strong emphasis on customer collaboration and responding to change.

326. Question: What is the primary goal of program resource management?

A) To track program schedule performance

B) To allocate resources to program activities efficiently

C) To manage program finances

D) To ensure program compliance with regulations

Answer: B) To allocate resources to program activities efficiently

Explanation: Program resource management focuses on allocating resources to program activities efficiently to meet program objectives.

327. Question: In program management, what does the term "Program Portfolio" refer to?

A) A collection of individual projects within a program

B) A visual representation of program stakeholders

C) A document outlining program benefits

D) A strategic collection of related programs and projects managed as a group

Answer: D) A strategic collection of related programs and projects managed as a group

Explanation: A Program Portfolio refers to a strategic collection of related programs and projects managed as a group to achieve overarching organizational objectives.

328. Question: What is the primary purpose of a Program Quality Management Plan?

A) To allocate resources to program activities

B) To track program schedule performance

C) To define how program quality will be planned, assured, and controlled

D) To create a detailed program budget

Answer: C) To define how program quality will be planned, assured, and controlled

Explanation: A Program Quality Management Plan defines how program quality will be planned, assured, and controlled to meet specified standards.

329. Question: Which program management role is responsible for securing funding and resources for the program?

A) Program Manager

B) Program Sponsor

C) Program Coordinator

D) Program Governance Board

Answer: B) Program Sponsor

Explanation: The Program Sponsor is responsible for securing funding and resources for the program and ensuring it aligns with organizational goals.

330. Question: What is the primary purpose of a Program Stakeholder Engagement Plan?

A) To allocate resources to program activities

B) To track program schedule performance

C) To document the strategy for engaging and managing program stakeholders

D) To create a detailed program budget

Answer: C) To document the strategy for engaging and managing program stakeholders

Explanation: A Program Stakeholder Engagement Plan is used to document the strategy for engaging and managing program stakeholders effectively.

331. Question: In program management, what does the term "Program Risk Tolerance" refer to?

A) The willingness to accept program risks

B) The program's budget allocation

C) The timeline for program delivery

D) The program's stakeholder engagement strategy

Answer: A) The willingness to accept program risks

Explanation: Program Risk Tolerance refers to the organization's or program's willingness to accept and tolerate certain levels of risk.

332. Question: What is the primary purpose of a Program Closure Report?

A) To allocate resources to program activities

B) To assess the realization of program benefits against expected outcomes

C) To track program financial performance

D) To create a detailed program budget

Answer: B) To assess the realization of program benefits against expected outcomes

Explanation: A Program Closure Report assesses the realization of program benefits against expected outcomes, summarizing the program's achievements.

333. Question: In program management, what does the term "Program Evaluation and Review Technique (PERT)" refer to?

A) A tool for tracking program finances

B) A process for identifying and managing program dependencies

C) A method for documenting program risks

D) A technique for estimating program durations based on optimistic, pessimistic, and most likely scenarios

Answer: D) A technique for estimating program durations based on optimistic, pessimistic, and most likely scenarios

Explanation: PERT is a technique used in program management to estimate program durations based on optimistic, pessimistic, and most likely scenarios, aiding in scheduling and planning.

334. Question: What is the primary focus of program stakeholder analysis?

A) To allocate resources to program activities

B) To track program schedule performance

C) To identify and understand the interests and influence of program stakeholders

D) To create a detailed program budget

Answer: C) To identify and understand the interests and influence of program stakeholders

Explanation: Program stakeholder analysis focuses on identifying and understanding the interests and influence of program stakeholders, facilitating effective stakeholder management.

335. Question: What is the primary purpose of a Program Governance Plan?

A) To allocate resources to program activities

B) To track program schedule performance

C) To document the program's governance structure and decision-making processes

D) To create a detailed program budget

Answer: C) To document the program's governance structure and decision-making processes

Explanation: A Program Governance Plan is used to document the program's governance structure and decision-making processes, ensuring clarity and transparency.

336. Question: In program management, what is the primary purpose of a Program Risk Mitigation Plan?

A) To allocate resources to program activities

B) To document and track program risks and their mitigation strategies

C) To assess program financial performance

D) To create a detailed program budget

Answer: B) To document and track program risks and their mitigation strategies

Explanation: A Program Risk Mitigation Plan is used to document and track program risks and their mitigation strategies to reduce potential negative impacts.

337. Question: What is the primary goal of program quality assurance?

A) To allocate resources to program activities

B) To assess program benefits realization

C) To ensure that program processes and activities conform to established standards

D) To track program financial performance

Answer: C) To ensure that program processes and activities conform to established standards

Explanation: Program quality assurance focuses on ensuring that program processes and activities conform to established standards, promoting quality throughout the program.

338. Question: What is the primary purpose of a Program Communication Plan?

A) To allocate resources to program activities

B) To track program schedule performance

C) To outline how program communication will be managed and executed

D) To create a detailed program budget

Answer: C) To outline how program communication will be managed and executed

Explanation: A Program Communication Plan outlines how program communication will be managed and executed, ensuring effective stakeholder communication.

339. Question: What is the primary goal of program stakeholder engagement?

A) To allocate resources to program activities

B) To assess program benefits realization

C) To build positive relationships and foster collaboration with program stakeholders

D) To create a detailed program budget

Answer: C) To build positive relationships and foster collaboration with program stakeholders

Explanation: The primary goal of program stakeholder engagement is to build positive relationships and foster collaboration with program stakeholders, promoting their active involvement in the program.

340. Question: What is the primary purpose of a Program Portfolio Management Office (PPMO)?

A) To allocate resources to program activities

B) To track program schedule performance

C) To provide centralized oversight, coordination, and support for multiple programs and their interdependencies

D) To create a detailed program budget

Answer: C) To provide centralized oversight, coordination, and support for multiple programs and their interdependencies

Explanation: A Program Portfolio Management Office (PPMO) provides centralized oversight, coordination, and support for multiple programs and their interdependencies within an organization.

PRACTICE TEST -3

341
. Question: What is the primary purpose of a Program Financial Management Plan?

A) To allocate resources to program activities

B) To assess program risks

C) To outline how program finances will be managed, monitored, and controlled

D) To create a detailed program schedule

Answer: C) To outline how program finances will be managed, monitored, and controlled

Explanation: A Program Financial Management Plan outlines how program finances will be managed, monitored, and controlled to ensure fiscal responsibility.

342. Question: Which program management role is responsible for aligning the program with the organization's strategic goals and objectives?

A) Program Manager

B) Program Sponsor

C) Program Coordinator

D) Program Governance Board

Answer: B) Program Sponsor

Explanation: The Program Sponsor is responsible for aligning the program with the organization's strategic goals and objectives.

343. Question: In program management, what does the term "Program Assurance" refer to?

A) A process for identifying program dependencies

B) A method for documenting program risks

C) An independent evaluation to ensure the program complies with standards and regulations

D) A tool for tracking program finances

Answer: C) An independent evaluation to ensure the program complies with standards and regulations

Explanation: Program Assurance involves an independent evaluation to ensure the program complies with standards and regulations, providing confidence in program delivery.

344. Question: What is the primary focus of program stakeholder analysis?

A) To allocate resources to program activities

B) To track program schedule performance

C) To identify and understand the interests and influence of program stakeholders

D) To create a detailed program budget

Answer: C) To identify and understand the interests and influence of program stakeholders

Explanation: Program stakeholder analysis focuses on identifying and understanding the interests and influence of program stakeholders, facilitating effective stakeholder management.

345. Question: Which program management approach is best suited for programs with a high degree of uncertainty and a need for frequent adaptation?

A) Traditional Program Management

B) Agile Program Management

C) Lean Program Management

D) Waterfall Program Management

Answer: B) Agile Program Management

Explanation: Agile Program Management is best suited for programs with a high degree of uncertainty and a need for frequent adaptation, as it emphasizes flexibility and responsiveness.

346. Question: What is the primary goal of program resource optimization?

A) To assess program risks

B) To allocate resources to program activities optimally

C) To manage program finances

D) To ensure program compliance with regulations

Answer: B) To allocate resources to program activities optimally

Explanation: The primary goal of program resource optimization is to allocate resources to program activities optimally, ensuring efficient resource utilization.

347. Question: In program management, what does the term "Program Dependency" refer to?

A) A tool for tracking program finances

B) A relationship between program activities or projects where one's success depends on the other

C) A method for documenting program risks

D) A technique for estimating program durations

Answer: B) A relationship between program activities or projects where one's success depends on the other

Explanation: A Program Dependency refers to a relationship between program activities or projects where one's success depends on the other, requiring coordination.

348. Question: What is the primary purpose of a Program Quality Assurance Plan?

A) To allocate resources to program activities

B) To assess program benefits realization

C) To define how program quality will be planned, assured, and controlled

D) To create a detailed program schedule

Answer: C) To define how program quality will be planned, assured, and controlled

Explanation: A Program Quality Assurance Plan defines how program quality will be planned, assured, and controlled to meet specified standards.

349. Question: Which program management role is responsible for providing direction and support to the program manager?

A) Program Manager

B) Program Sponsor

C) Program Coordinator

D) Program Governance Board

Answer: D) Program Governance Board

Explanation: The Program Governance Board provides direction and support to the program manager, ensuring alignment with organizational objectives.

350. Question: What is the primary purpose of a Program Stakeholder Engagement Plan?

A) To allocate resources to program activities

B) To track program schedule performance

C) To document the strategy for engaging and managing program stakeholders

D) To create a detailed program budget

Answer: C) To document the strategy for engaging and managing program stakeholders

Explanation: A Program Stakeholder Engagement Plan is used to document the strategy for engaging and managing program stakeholders effectively.

351. Question: In program management, what does the term "Program Risk Threshold" refer to?

A) The willingness to accept program risks

B) The program's budget allocation

C) The timeline for program delivery

D) The maximum acceptable level of risk for the program

Answer: D) The maximum acceptable level of risk for the program

Explanation: Program Risk Threshold refers to the maximum acceptable level of risk that the program is willing to tolerate.

352. Question: What is the primary purpose of a Program Closure Report?

A) To allocate resources to program activities

B) To assess the realization of program benefits against expected outcomes

C) To track program financial performance

D) To create a detailed program budget

Answer: B) To assess the realization of program benefits against expected outcomes

Explanation: A Program Closure Report assesses the realization of program benefits against expected outcomes, summarizing the program's achievements.

353. Question: In program management, what does the term "Program Evaluation and Review Technique (PERT)" refer to?

A) A tool for tracking program finances

B) A process for identifying and managing program dependencies

C) A method for documenting program risks

D) A technique for estimating program durations based on optimistic, pessimistic, and most likely scenarios

Answer: D) A technique for estimating program durations based on optimistic, pessimistic, and most likely scenarios

Explanation: PERT is a technique used in program management to estimate program durations based on optimistic, pessimistic, and most likely scenarios, aiding in scheduling and planning.

354. Question: What is the primary focus of program stakeholder communication?

A) To allocate resources to program activities

B) To track program schedule performance

C) To provide relevant and timely information to program stakeholders

D) To manage program finances

Answer: C) To provide relevant and timely information to program stakeholders

Explanation: The primary goal of program stakeholder communication is to provide relevant and timely information to program stakeholders, ensuring they are well-informed and engaged in program activities.

355. Question: What is the primary purpose of a Program Governance Plan?

A) To allocate resources to program activities

B) To track program schedule performance

C) To document the program's governance structure and decision-making processes

D) To create a detailed program budget

Answer: C) To document the program's governance structure and decision-making processes

Explanation: A Program Governance Plan is used to document the program's governance structure and decision-making processes, ensuring clarity and transparency.

356. Question: In program management, what is the primary purpose of a Program Risk Mitigation Plan?

A) To allocate resources to program activities

B) To document and track program risks and their mitigation strategies

C) To assess program financial performance

D) To create a detailed program budget

Answer: B) To document and track program risks and their mitigation strategies

Explanation: A Program Risk Mitigation Plan is used to document and track program risks and their mitigation strategies to reduce potential negative impacts.

357. Question: What is the primary goal of program quality assurance?

A) To allocate resources to program activities

B) To assess program benefits realization

C) To ensure that program processes and activities conform to established standards

D) To track program financial performance

Answer: C) To ensure that program processes and activities conform to established standards

Explanation: Program quality assurance focuses on ensuring that program processes and activities conform to established standards, promoting quality throughout the program.

358. Question: What is the primary purpose of a Program Communication Plan?

A) To allocate resources to program activities

B) To track program schedule performance

C) To outline how program communication will be managed and executed

D) To create a detailed program budget

Answer: C) To outline how program communication will be managed and executed

Explanation: A Program Communication Plan outlines how program communication will be managed and executed, ensuring effective stakeholder communication.

359. Question: What is the primary goal of program stakeholder engagement?

A) To allocate resources to program activities

B) To assess program benefits realization

C) To build positive relationships and foster collaboration with program stakeholders

D) To create a detailed program budget

Answer: C) To build positive relationships and foster collaboration with program stakeholders

Explanation: The primary goal of program stakeholder engagement is to build positive relationships and foster collaboration with program stakeholders, promoting their active involvement in the program.

360. Question: What is the primary purpose of a Program Portfolio Management Office (PPMO)?

A) To allocate resources to program activities

B) To track program schedule performance

C) To provide centralized oversight, coordination, and support for multiple programs and their interdependencies

D) To create a detailed program budget

Answer: C) To provide centralized oversight, coordination, and support for multiple programs and their interdependencies

Explanation: A Program Portfolio Management Office (PPMO) provides centralized oversight, coordination, and support for multiple programs and their interdependencies within an organization.

361. Question: What is the primary purpose of a Program Risk Management Plan?

A) To allocate resources to program activities

B) To track program schedule performance

C) To outline how program risks will be identified, assessed, and managed

D) To create a detailed program budget

Answer: C) To outline how program risks will be identified, assessed, and managed

Explanation: A Program Risk Management Plan outlines how program risks will be identified, assessed, and managed throughout the program's lifecycle.

362. Question: Which program management role is responsible for defining and managing program scope?

A) Program Manager

B) Program Sponsor

C) Program Coordinator

D) Program Governance Board

Answer: A) Program Manager

Explanation: The Program Manager is responsible for defining and managing program scope, ensuring that program objectives are met.

363. Question: In program management, what does the term "Program Assurance" refer to?

A) A tool for tracking program finances

B) A process for identifying program dependencies

C) An independent evaluation to ensure the program complies with standards and regulations

D) A method for documenting program risks

Answer: C) An independent evaluation to ensure the program complies with standards and regulations

Explanation: Program Assurance involves an independent evaluation to ensure the program complies with standards and regulations, providing confidence in program delivery.

364. Question: What is the primary focus of program stakeholder analysis?

A) To allocate resources to program activities

B) To track program schedule performance

C) To identify and understand the interests and influence of program stakeholders

D) To create a detailed program budget

Answer: C) To identify and understand the interests and influence of program stakeholders

Explanation: Program stakeholder analysis focuses on identifying and understanding the interests and influence of program stakeholders, facilitating effective stakeholder management.

365. Question: Which program management approach emphasizes delivering value incrementally and frequently, with a focus on customer collaboration?

A) Traditional Program Management

B) Agile Program Management

C) Lean Program Management

D) Waterfall Program Management

Answer: B) Agile Program Management

Explanation: Agile Program Management focuses on delivering value incrementally and frequently, with a strong emphasis on customer collaboration and responding to change.

366. Question: What is the primary goal of program resource optimization?

A) To assess program risks

B) To allocate resources to program activities optimally

C) To manage program finances

D) To ensure program compliance with regulations

Answer: B) To allocate resources to program activities optimally

Explanation: The primary goal of program resource optimization is to allocate resources to program activities optimally, ensuring efficient resource utilization.

367. Question: In program management, what does the term "Program Dependency" refer to?

A) A tool for tracking program finances

B) A relationship between program activities or projects where one's success depends on the other

C) A method for documenting program risks

D) A technique for estimating program durations

Answer: B) A relationship between program activities or projects where one's success depends on the other

Explanation: A Program Dependency refers to a relationship between program activities or projects where one's success depends on the other, requiring coordination.

368. Question: What is the primary purpose of a Program Quality Assurance Plan?

A) To allocate resources to program activities

B) To assess program benefits realization

C) To define how program quality will be planned, assured, and controlled

D) To create a detailed program schedule

Answer: C) To define how program quality will be planned, assured, and controlled

Explanation: A Program Quality Assurance Plan defines how program quality will be planned, assured, and controlled to meet specified standards.

369. Question: Which program management role is responsible for providing direction and support to the program manager?

A) Program Manager

B) Program Sponsor

C) Program Coordinator

D) Program Governance Board

Answer: D) Program Governance Board

Explanation: The Program Governance Board provides direction and support to the program manager, ensuring alignment with organizational objectives.

370. Question: What is the primary purpose of a Program Stakeholder Engagement Plan?

A) To allocate resources to program activities

B) To track program schedule performance

C) To document the strategy for engaging and managing program stakeholders

D) To create a detailed program budget

Answer: C) To document the strategy for engaging and managing program stakeholders

Explanation: A Program Stakeholder Engagement Plan is used to document the strategy for engaging and managing program stakeholders effectively.

371. Question: In program management, what does the term "Program Risk Threshold" refer to?

A) The willingness to accept program risks

B) The program's budget allocation

C) The timeline for program delivery

D) The maximum acceptable level of risk for the program

Answer: D) The maximum acceptable level of risk for the program

Explanation: Program Risk Threshold refers to the maximum acceptable level of risk that the program is willing to tolerate.

372. Question: What is the primary purpose of a Program Closure Report?

A) To allocate resources to program activities

B) To assess the realization of program benefits against expected outcomes

C) To track program financial performance

D) To create a detailed program budget

Answer: B) To assess the realization of program benefits against expected outcomes

Explanation: A Program Closure Report assesses the realization of program benefits against expected outcomes, summarizing the program's achievements.

373. Question: In program management, what does the term "Program Evaluation and Review Technique (PERT)" refer to?

A) A tool for tracking program finances

B) A process for identifying and managing program dependencies

C) A method for documenting program risks

D) A technique for estimating program durations based on optimistic, pessimistic, and most likely scenarios

Answer: D) A technique for estimating program durations based on optimistic, pessimistic, and most likely scenarios

Explanation: PERT is a technique used in program management to estimate program durations based on optimistic, pessimistic, and most likely scenarios, aiding in scheduling and planning.

374. Question: What is the primary focus of program stakeholder communication?

A) To allocate resources to program activities

B) To track program schedule performance

C) To provide relevant and timely information to program stakeholders

D) To manage program finances

Answer: C) To provide relevant and timely information to program stakeholders

Explanation: The primary goal of program stakeholder communication is to provide relevant and timely information to program stakeholders, ensuring they are well-informed and engaged in program activities.

375. Question: What is the primary purpose of a Program Governance Plan?

A) To allocate resources to program activities

B) To track program schedule performance

C) To document the program's governance structure and decision-making processes

D) To create a detailed program budget

Answer: C) To document the program's governance structure and decision-making processes

Explanation: A Program Governance Plan is used to document the program's governance structure and decision-making processes, ensuring clarity and transparency.

376. Question: In program management, what is the primary purpose of a Program Risk Mitigation Plan?

A) To allocate resources to program activities

B) To document and track program risks and their mitigation strategies

C) To assess program financial performance

D) To create a detailed program budget

Answer: B) To document and track program risks and their mitigation strategies

Explanation: A Program Risk Mitigation Plan is used to document and track program risks and their mitigation strategies to reduce potential negative impacts.

377. Question: What is the primary goal of program quality assurance?

A) To allocate resources to program activities

B) To assess program benefits realization

C) To ensure that program processes and activities conform to established standards

D) To track program financial performance

Answer: C) To ensure that program processes and activities conform to established standards

Explanation: Program quality assurance focuses on ensuring that program processes and activities conform to established standards, promoting quality throughout the program.

378. Question: What is the primary purpose of a Program Communication Plan?

A) To allocate resources to program activities

B) To track program schedule performance

C) To outline how program communication will be managed and executed

D) To create a detailed program budget

Answer: C) To outline how program communication will be managed and executed

Explanation: A Program Communication Plan outlines how program communication will be managed and executed, ensuring effective stakeholder communication.

379. Question: What is the primary goal of program stakeholder engagement?

A) To allocate resources to program activities

B) To assess program benefits realization

C) To build positive relationships and foster collaboration with program stakeholders

D) To create a detailed program budget

Answer: C) To build positive relationships and foster collaboration with program stakeholders

Explanation: The primary goal of program stakeholder engagement is to build positive relationships and foster collaboration with program stakeholders, promoting their active involvement in the program.

380. Question: What is the primary purpose of a Program Portfolio Management Office (PPMO)?

A) To allocate resources to program activities

B) To track program schedule performance

C) To provide centralized oversight, coordination, and support for multiple programs and their interdependencies

D) To create a detailed program budget

Answer: C) To provide centralized oversight, coordination, and support for multiple programs and their interdependencies

Explanation: A Program Portfolio Management Office (PPMO) provides centralized oversight, coordination, and support for multiple programs and their interdependencies within an organization.

381. Question: What is the primary purpose of a Program Stakeholder Register?

A) To allocate resources to program activities

B) To track program schedule performance

C) To document and categorize program stakeholders and their interests

D) To create a detailed program budget

Answer: C) To document and categorize program stakeholders and their interests

Explanation: A Program Stakeholder Register is used to document and categorize program stakeholders and their interests, aiding in effective stakeholder management.

382. Question: In program management, what does the term "Program Risk Appetite" refer to?

A) The willingness to accept program risks

B) The program's budget allocation

C) The timeline for program delivery

D) The maximum acceptable level of program scope

Answer: A) The willingness to accept program risks

Explanation: Program Risk Appetite refers to the organization's or program's willingness to accept and tolerate risks in pursuit of its objectives.

383. Question: Which program management role is responsible for ensuring that program activities are completed on time, within scope, and on budget?

A) Program Manager

B) Program Sponsor

C) Program Coordinator

D) Program Governance Board

Answer: A) Program Manager

Explanation: The Program Manager is responsible for ensuring that program activities are completed on time, within scope, and on budget.

384. Question: What is the primary focus of program benefits management?

A) To allocate resources to program activities

B) To track program schedule performance

C) To identify, define, and realize program benefits

D) To create a detailed program budget

Answer: C) To identify, define, and realize program benefits

Explanation: The primary focus of program benefits management is to identify, define, and realize program benefits to maximize value.

385. Question: Which program management approach emphasizes the elimination of waste and maximizing customer value while minimizing resources?

A) Traditional Program Management

B) Agile Program Management

C) Lean Program Management

D) Waterfall Program Management

Answer: C) Lean Program Management

Explanation: Lean Program Management emphasizes the elimination of waste and maximizing customer value while minimizing resources.

386. Question: What is the primary goal of program financial control?

A) To assess program risks

B) To allocate resources to program activities optimally

C) To manage program finances effectively

D) To ensure program compliance with regulations

Answer: C) To manage program finances effectively

Explanation: The primary goal of program financial control is to manage program finances effectively, ensuring that resources are used efficiently.

387. Question: In program management, what does the term "Program Dependency Mapping" refer to?

A) A tool for tracking program finances

B) A process for identifying and managing program dependencies

C) A method for documenting program risks

D) A technique for estimating program durations

Answer: B) A process for identifying and managing program dependencies

Explanation: Program Dependency Mapping involves the process of identifying and managing program dependencies to ensure coordination and successful execution.

388. Question: What is the primary purpose of a Program Governance Framework?

A) To allocate resources to program activities

B) To track program schedule performance

C) To establish the structure, roles, and responsibilities for program governance

D) To create a detailed program budget

Answer: C) To establish the structure, roles, and responsibilities for program governance

Explanation: A Program Governance Framework is used to establish the structure, roles, and responsibilities for program governance, ensuring effective oversight.

389. Question: Which program management role is responsible for providing funding and strategic alignment to the program?

A) Program Manager

B) Program Sponsor

C) Program Coordinator

D) Program Governance Board

Answer: B) Program Sponsor

Explanation: The Program Sponsor is responsible for providing funding and strategic alignment to the program.

390. Question: What is the primary purpose of a Program Risk Register?

A) To allocate resources to program activities

B) To document and track program risks and their potential impact

C) To assess program benefits realization

D) To create a detailed program schedule

Answer: B) To document and track program risks and their potential impact

Explanation: A Program Risk Register is used to document and track program risks and their potential impact on the program's objectives.

391. Question: In program management, what does the term "Program Performance Measurement" refer to?

A) A tool for tracking program finances

B) A process for identifying and managing program dependencies

C) A method for documenting program risks

D) The tracking and evaluation of program progress and results

Answer: D) The tracking and evaluation of program progress and results

Explanation: Program Performance Measurement involves the tracking and evaluation of program progress and results to ensure alignment with objectives.

392. Question: What is the primary focus of program stakeholder engagement?

A) To allocate resources to program activities

B) To assess program benefits realization

C) To build positive relationships and foster collaboration with program stakeholders

D) To create a detailed program budget

Answer: C) To build positive relationships and foster collaboration with program stakeholders

Explanation: The primary goal of program stakeholder engagement is to build positive relationships and foster collaboration with program stakeholders, promoting their active involvement in the program.

393. Question: What is the primary purpose of a Program Portfolio Management Office (PPMO)?

A) To allocate resources to program activities

B) To track program schedule performance

C) To provide centralized oversight, coordination, and support for multiple programs and their interdependencies

D) To create a detailed program budget

Answer: C) To provide centralized oversight, coordination, and support for multiple programs and their interdependencies

Explanation: A Program Portfolio Management Office (PPMO) provides centralized oversight, coordination, and support for multiple programs and their interdependencies within an organization.

394. Question: What is the primary goal of program stakeholder communication?

A) To allocate resources to program activities

B) To track program schedule performance

C) To provide relevant and timely information to program stakeholders

D) To manage program finances

Answer: C) To provide relevant and timely information to program stakeholders

Explanation: The primary goal of program stakeholder communication is to provide relevant and timely information to program stakeholders, ensuring they are well-informed and engaged in program activities.

395. Question: What is the primary purpose of a Program Benefit Realization Plan?

A) To allocate resources to program activities

B) To track program schedule performance

C) To outline how program benefits will be identified, measured, and realized

D) To create a detailed program budget

Answer: C) To outline how program benefits will be identified, measured, and realized

Explanation: A Program Benefit Realization Plan outlines how program benefits will be identified, measured, and realized, ensuring that program objectives are met.

396. Question: In program management, what does the term "Program Dependency Analysis" refer to?

A) A tool for tracking program finances

B) A process for identifying and managing program dependencies

C) A method for documenting program risks

D) A technique for estimating program durations

Answer: B) A process for identifying and managing program dependencies

Explanation: Program Dependency Analysis involves the process of identifying and managing program dependencies to ensure coordination and successful execution.

397. Question: What is the primary purpose of a Program Stakeholder Communication Plan?

A) To allocate resources to program activities

B) To track program schedule performance

C) To outline how program communication with stakeholders will be planned and executed

D) To create a detailed program budget

Answer: C) To outline how program communication with stakeholders will be planned and executed

Explanation: A Program Stakeholder Communication Plan outlines how program communication with stakeholders will be planned and executed, ensuring effective engagement.

398. Question: What is the primary focus of program resource allocation?

A) To assess program risks

B) To allocate resources to program activities optimally

C) To manage program finances

D) To ensure program compliance with regulations

Answer: B) To allocate resources to program activities optimally

Explanation: The primary focus of program resource allocation is to allocate resources to program activities optimally, ensuring efficient resource utilization.

399. Question: In program management, what does the term "Program Risk Mitigation" refer to?

A) A tool for tracking program finances

B) A process for identifying and managing program dependencies

C) Strategies and actions taken to reduce the impact of program risks

D) A technique for estimating program durations

Answer: C) Strategies and actions taken to reduce the impact of program risks

Explanation: Program Risk Mitigation involves strategies and actions taken to reduce the impact of program risks, helping to minimize potential negative consequences.

400. Question: What is the primary purpose of a Program Benefits Dependency Matrix?

A) To allocate resources to program activities

B) To track program schedule performance

C) To document and analyze the dependencies between program benefits

D) To create a detailed program budget

Answer: C) To document and analyze the dependencies between program benefits

Explanation: A Program Benefits Dependency Matrix is used to document and analyze the dependencies between program benefits, ensuring a clear understanding of how they relate to each other.

401. Question: What is the primary purpose of a Program Risk Assessment?

A) To allocate resources to program activities

B) To track program schedule performance

C) To evaluate the potential impact of risks on program objectives

D) To create a detailed program budget

Answer: C) To evaluate the potential impact of risks on program objectives

Explanation: A Program Risk Assessment is conducted to evaluate the potential impact of risks on program objectives, helping to prioritize risk mitigation efforts.

402. Question: In program management, what is the primary purpose of a Program Benefits Realization Plan?

A) To allocate resources to program activities

B) To track program schedule performance

C) To outline how program benefits will be identified, measured, and realized

D) To create a detailed program budget

Answer: C) To outline how program benefits will be identified, measured, and realized

Explanation: A Program Benefits Realization Plan outlines how program benefits will be identified, measured, and realized to achieve program objectives.

403. Question: Which program management role is responsible for ensuring that program governance aligns with organizational strategy and objectives?

A) Program Manager

B) Program Sponsor

C) Program Coordinator

D) Program Governance Board

Answer: B) Program Sponsor

Explanation: The Program Sponsor is responsible for ensuring that program governance aligns with organizational strategy and objectives.

404. Question: What is the primary focus of program performance measurement?

A) To allocate resources to program activities

B) To track program schedule performance

C) To monitor and assess program progress and results

D) To create a detailed program budget

Answer: C) To monitor and assess program progress and results

Explanation: The primary focus of program performance measurement is to monitor and assess program progress and results to ensure alignment with program objectives.

405. Question: Which program management approach emphasizes delivering value in stages while adapting to changing requirements?

A) Traditional Program Management

B) Agile Program Management

C) Lean Program Management

D) Waterfall Program Management

Answer: B) Agile Program Management

Explanation: Agile Program Management emphasizes delivering value in stages while adapting to changing requirements and customer feedback.

406. Question: What is the primary goal of program financial control?

A) To assess program risks

B) To allocate resources to program activities optimally

C) To manage program finances effectively

D) To ensure program compliance with regulations

Answer: C) To manage program finances effectively

Explanation: The primary goal of program financial control is to manage program finances effectively, ensuring that resources are used efficiently.

407. Question: In program management, what does the term "Program Dependency Analysis" refer to?

A) A tool for tracking program finances

B) A process for identifying and managing program dependencies

C) A method for documenting program risks

D) A technique for estimating program durations

Answer: B) A process for identifying and managing program dependencies

Explanation: Program Dependency Analysis involves the process of identifying and managing program dependencies to ensure coordination and successful execution.

408. Question: What is the primary purpose of a Program Governance Framework?

A) To allocate resources to program activities

B) To track program schedule performance

C) To establish the structure, roles, and responsibilities for program governance

D) To create a detailed program budget

Answer: C) To establish the structure, roles, and responsibilities for program governance

Explanation: A Program Governance Framework is used to establish the structure, roles, and responsibilities for program governance, ensuring effective oversight.

409. Question: Which program management role is responsible for providing funding, resources, and strategic alignment to the program?

A) Program Manager

B) Program Sponsor

C) Program Coordinator

D) Program Governance Board

Answer: B) Program Sponsor

Explanation: The Program Sponsor is responsible for providing funding, resources, and strategic alignment to the program.

410. Question: What is the primary purpose of a Program Risk Register?

A) To allocate resources to program activities

B) To document and track program risks and their potential impact

C) To assess program benefits realization

D) To create a detailed program schedule

Answer: B) To document and track program risks and their potential impact

Explanation: A Program Risk Register is used to document and track program risks and their potential impact on the program's objectives.

411. Question: In program management, what does the term "Program Performance Measurement" refer to?

A) A tool for tracking program finances

B) A process for identifying and managing program dependencies

C) A method for documenting program risks

D) The tracking and evaluation of program progress and results

Answer: D) The tracking and evaluation of program progress and results

Explanation: Program Performance Measurement involves the tracking and evaluation of program progress and results to ensure alignment with objectives.

412. Question: What is the primary focus of program stakeholder engagement?

A) To allocate resources to program activities

B) To assess program benefits realization

C) To build positive relationships and foster collaboration with program stakeholders

D) To create a detailed program budget

Answer: C) To build positive relationships and foster collaboration with program stakeholders

Explanation: The primary goal of program stakeholder engagement is to build positive relationships and foster collaboration with program stakeholders, promoting their active involvement in the program.

413. Question: What is the primary purpose of a Program Benefit Dependency Matrix?

A) To allocate resources to program activities

B) To track program schedule performance

C) To document and analyze the dependencies between program benefits

D) To create a detailed program budget

Answer: C) To document and analyze the dependencies between program benefits

Explanation: A Program Benefit Dependency Matrix is used to document and analyze the dependencies between program benefits, ensuring a clear understanding of how they relate to each other.

414. Question: In program management, what does the term "Program Risk Threshold" refer to?

A) The willingness to accept program risks

B) The program's budget allocation

C) The timeline for program delivery

D) The maximum acceptable level of risk for the program

Answer: D) The maximum acceptable level of risk for the program

Explanation: Program Risk Threshold refers to the maximum acceptable level of risk that the program is willing to tolerate.

415. Question: What is the primary purpose of a Program Governance Charter?

A) To allocate resources to program activities

B) To track program schedule performance

C) To define the program's governance framework, authority, and responsibilities

D) To create a detailed program budget

Answer: C) To define the program's governance framework, authority, and responsibilities

Explanation: A Program Governance Charter is used to define the program's governance framework, authority, and responsibilities, ensuring clear governance guidelines.

416. Question: What is the primary goal of program stakeholder communication?

A) To allocate resources to program activities

B) To track program schedule performance

C) To provide relevant and timely information to program stakeholders

D) To manage program finances

Answer: C) To provide relevant and timely information to program stakeholders

Explanation: The primary goal of program stakeholder communication is to provide relevant and timely information to program stakeholders, ensuring they are well-informed and engaged in program activities.

417. Question: In program management, what does the term "Program Governance Board" typically consist of?

A) Program Managers and Sponsors

B) Program Team Members

C) External Stakeholders

D) Senior Management and Executives

Answer: D) Senior Management and Executives

Explanation: A Program Governance Board typically consists of senior management and executives who provide oversight and decision-making authority for the program.

418. Question: What is the primary purpose of a Program Scope Statement?

A) To allocate resources to program activities

B) To track program schedule performance

C) To define the program's scope, objectives, and deliverables

D) To create a detailed program budget

Answer: C) To define the program's scope, objectives, and deliverables

Explanation: A Program Scope Statement is used to define the program's scope, objectives, and deliverables, providing clarity on what the program will achieve.

419. Question: What is the primary purpose of a Program Change Control Process?

A) To allocate resources to program activities

B) To track program schedule performance

C) To manage and document changes to the program's scope, schedule, and budget

D) To create a detailed program schedule

Answer: C) To manage and document changes to the program's scope, schedule, and budget

Explanation: A Program Change Control Process is used to manage and document changes to the program's scope, schedule, and budget, ensuring proper governance of changes.

420. Question: What is the primary goal of program risk management?

A) To allocate resources to program activities

B) To assess program benefits realization

C) To identify, assess, and mitigate risks that may impact program objectives

D) To create a detailed program budget

Answer: C) To identify, assess, and mitigate risks that may impact program objectives

Explanation: The primary goal of program risk management is to identify, assess, and mitigate risks that may impact program objectives, minimizing potential negative impacts.

421. Question: In program management, what does the term "Program Governance Framework" primarily establish?

A) Detailed program budget

B) Program scope and objectives

C) Structure, roles, and responsibilities for program governance

D) Program risk assessment plan

Answer: C) Structure, roles, and responsibilities for program governance

Explanation: A Program Governance Framework primarily establishes the structure, roles, and responsibilities for program governance, ensuring effective oversight.

422. Question: What is the primary goal of program quality assurance?

A) To allocate resources to program activities

B) To assess program benefits realization

C) To ensure that program processes and activities conform to established standards

D) To create a detailed program schedule

Answer: C) To ensure that program processes and activities conform to established standards

Explanation: Program quality assurance aims to ensure that program processes and activities conform to established standards, promoting quality throughout the program.

423. Question: What is the primary purpose of a Program Risk Mitigation Plan?

A) To allocate resources to program activities

B) To document and track program risks and their mitigation strategies

C) To assess program financial performance

D) To create a detailed program budget

Answer: B) To document and track program risks and their mitigation strategies

Explanation: A Program Risk Mitigation Plan is used to document and track program risks and their mitigation strategies, reducing potential negative impacts.

424. Question: Which program management role is responsible for providing funding and strategic alignment to the program?

A) Program Manager

B) Program Sponsor

C) Program Coordinator

D) Program Governance Board

Answer: B) Program Sponsor

Explanation: The Program Sponsor is responsible for providing funding and strategic alignment to the program.

425. Question: What is the primary focus of program resource allocation?

A) To assess program risks

B) To allocate resources to program activities optimally

C) To manage program finances

D) To ensure program compliance with regulations

Answer: B) To allocate resources to program activities optimally

Explanation: The primary focus of program resource allocation is to allocate resources to program activities optimally, ensuring efficient resource utilization.

426. Question: In program management, what does the term "Program Dependency Mapping" refer to?

A) A tool for tracking program finances

B) A process for identifying and managing program dependencies

C) A method for documenting program risks

D) A technique for estimating program durations

Answer: B) A process for identifying and managing program dependencies

Explanation: Program Dependency Mapping involves the process of identifying and managing program dependencies to ensure coordination and successful execution.

427. Question: What is the primary purpose of a Program Communication Plan?

A) To allocate resources to program activities

B) To track program schedule performance

C) To outline how program communication will be managed and executed

D) To create a detailed program budget

Answer: C) To outline how program communication will be managed and executed

Explanation: A Program Communication Plan outlines how program communication will be managed and executed, ensuring effective stakeholder communication.

428. Question: What is the primary goal of program stakeholder engagement?

A) To allocate resources to program activities

B) To assess program benefits realization

C) To build positive relationships and foster collaboration with program stakeholders

D) To create a detailed program budget

Answer: C) To build positive relationships and foster collaboration with program stakeholders

Explanation: The primary goal of program stakeholder engagement is to build positive relationships and foster collaboration with program stakeholders, promoting their active involvement in the program.

429. Question: What is the primary purpose of a Program Portfolio Management Office (PPMO)?

A) To allocate resources to program activities

B) To track program schedule performance

C) To provide centralized oversight, coordination, and support for multiple programs and their interdependencies

D) To create a detailed program budget

Answer: C) To provide centralized oversight, coordination, and support for multiple programs and their interdependencies

Explanation: A Program Portfolio Management Office (PPMO) provides centralized oversight, coordination, and support for multiple programs and their interdependencies within an organization.

430. Question: What is the primary goal of program stakeholder communication?

A) To allocate resources to program activities

B) To track program schedule performance

C) To provide relevant and timely information to program stakeholders

D) To manage program finances

Answer: C) To provide relevant and timely information to program stakeholders

Explanation: The primary goal of program stakeholder communication is to provide relevant and timely information to program stakeholders, ensuring they are well-informed and engaged in program activities.

431. Question: What is the primary purpose of a Program Benefit Realization Plan?

A) To allocate resources to program activities

B) To track program schedule performance

C) To outline how program benefits will be identified, measured, and realized

D) To create a detailed program budget

Answer: C) To outline how program benefits will be identified, measured, and realized

Explanation: A Program Benefit Realization Plan outlines how program benefits will be identified, measured, and realized, ensuring that program objectives are met.

432. Question: In program management, what does the term "Program Dependency Analysis" refer to?

A) A tool for tracking program finances

B) A process for identifying and managing program dependencies

C) A method for documenting program risks

D) A technique for estimating program durations

Answer: B) A process for identifying and managing program dependencies

Explanation: Program Dependency Analysis involves the process of identifying and managing program dependencies to ensure coordination and successful execution.

433. Question: What is the primary purpose of a Program Stakeholder Communication Plan?

A) To allocate resources to program activities

B) To track program schedule performance

C) To outline how program communication with stakeholders will be planned and executed

D) To create a detailed program budget

Answer: C) To outline how program communication with stakeholders will be planned and executed

Explanation: A Program Stakeholder Communication Plan outlines how program communication with stakeholders will be planned and executed, ensuring effective engagement.

434. Question: What is the primary focus of program resource allocation?

A) To assess program risks

B) To allocate resources to program activities optimally

C) To manage program finances

D) To ensure program compliance with regulations

Answer: B) To allocate resources to program activities optimally

Explanation: The primary focus of program resource allocation is to allocate resources to program activities optimally, ensuring efficient resource utilization.

435. Question: In program management, what does the term "Program Risk Mitigation" refer to?

A) A tool for tracking program finances

B) A process for identifying and managing program dependencies

C) Strategies and actions taken to reduce the impact of program risks

D) A technique for estimating program durations

Answer: C) Strategies and actions taken to reduce the impact of program risks

Explanation: Program Risk Mitigation involves strategies and actions taken to reduce the impact of program risks, helping to minimize potential negative consequences.

436. Question: What is the primary purpose of a Program Benefits Dependency Matrix?

A) To allocate resources to program activities

B) To track program schedule performance

C) To document and analyze the dependencies between program benefits

D) To create a detailed program budget

Answer: C) To document and analyze the dependencies between program benefits

Explanation: A Program Benefits Dependency Matrix is used to document and analyze the dependencies between program benefits, ensuring a clear understanding of how they relate to each other.

437. Question: In program management, what does the term "Program Benefits Realization" refer to?

A) The allocation of resources to program activities

B) The measurement of program schedule performance

C) The process of identifying, tracking, and realizing program benefits

D) The creation of a detailed program budget

Answer: C) The process of identifying, tracking, and realizing program benefits

Explanation: Program Benefits Realization refers to the process of identifying, tracking, and realizing program benefits to achieve program objectives.

438. Question: What is the primary purpose of a Program Governance Charter?

A) To allocate resources to program activities

B) To track program schedule performance

C) To define the program's governance framework, authority, and responsibilities

D) To create a detailed program budget

Answer: C) To define the program's governance framework, authority, and responsibilities

Explanation: A Program Governance Charter is used to define the program's governance framework, authority, and responsibilities, ensuring clear governance guidelines.

439. Question: What is the primary focus of program stakeholder engagement?

A) To allocate resources to program activities

B) To assess program benefits realization

C) To build positive relationships and foster collaboration with program stakeholders

D) To create a detailed program budget

Answer: C) To build positive relationships and foster collaboration with program stakeholders

Explanation: The primary focus of program stakeholder engagement is to build positive relationships and foster collaboration with program stakeholders, promoting their active involvement in the program.

440. Question: What is the primary purpose of a Program Benefits Dependency Matrix?

A) To allocate resources to program activities

B) To track program schedule performance

C) To document and analyze the dependencies between program benefits

D) To create a detailed program budget

Answer: C) To document and analyze the dependencies between program benefits

Explanation: A Program Benefit Dependency Matrix is used to document and analyze the dependencies between program benefits, ensuring a clear understanding of how they relate to each other.

441. Question: What is the primary purpose of a Program Governance Framework?

A) To allocate resources to program activities

B) To define the program's scope and objectives

C) To establish the structure, roles, and responsibilities for program governance

D) To create a detailed program schedule

Answer: C) To establish the structure, roles, and responsibilities for program governance

Explanation: A Program Governance Framework is used to establish the structure, roles, and responsibilities for program governance, ensuring effective oversight.

442. Question: What is the primary goal of program quality management?

A) To allocate resources to program activities

B) To assess program benefits realization

C) To ensure that program processes and deliverables meet established quality standards

D) To create a detailed program budget

Answer: C) To ensure that program processes and deliverables meet established quality standards

Explanation: The primary goal of program quality management is to ensure that program processes and deliverables meet established quality standards, promoting quality throughout the program.

443. Question: What is the primary purpose of a Program Risk Mitigation Plan?

A) To allocate resources to program activities

B) To document and track program risks and their potential impact

C) To assess program financial performance

D) To create a detailed program schedule

Answer: B) To document and track program risks and their potential impact

Explanation: A Program Risk Mitigation Plan is used to document and track program risks and their potential impact on the program's objectives.

444. Question: Which program management role is responsible for providing funding, resources, and strategic alignment to the program?

A) Program Manager

B) Program Sponsor

C) Program Coordinator

D) Program Governance Board

Answer: B) Program Sponsor

Explanation: The Program Sponsor is responsible for providing funding, resources, and strategic alignment to the program.

445. Question: What is the primary focus of program resource allocation?

A) To assess program risks

B) To allocate resources to program activities optimally

C) To manage program finances

D) To ensure program compliance with regulations

Answer: B) To allocate resources to program activities optimally

Explanation: The primary focus of program resource allocation is to allocate resources to program activities optimally, ensuring efficient resource utilization.

446. Question: In program management, what does the term "Program Dependency Analysis" refer to?

A) A tool for tracking program finances

B) A process for identifying and managing program dependencies

C) A method for documenting program risks

D) A technique for estimating program durations

Answer: B) A process for identifying and managing program dependencies

Explanation: Program Dependency Analysis involves the process of identifying and managing program dependencies to ensure coordination and successful execution.

447. Question: What is the primary purpose of a Program Communication Plan?

A) To allocate resources to program activities

B) To track program schedule performance

C) To outline how program communication will be managed and executed

D) To create a detailed program budget

Answer: C) To outline how program communication will be managed and executed

Explanation: A Program Communication Plan outlines how program communication will be managed and executed, ensuring effective stakeholder communication.

448. Question: What is the primary goal of program stakeholder engagement?

A) To allocate resources to program activities

B) To assess program benefits realization

C) To build positive relationships and foster collaboration with program stakeholders

D) To create a detailed program budget

Answer: C) To build positive relationships and foster collaboration with program stakeholders

Explanation: The primary goal of program stakeholder engagement is to build positive relationships and foster collaboration with program stakeholders, promoting their active involvement in the program.

449. Question: What is the primary purpose of a Program Portfolio Management Office (PPMO)?

A) To allocate resources to program activities

B) To track program schedule performance

C) To provide centralized oversight, coordination, and support for multiple programs and their interdependencies

D) To create a detailed program budget

Answer: C) To provide centralized oversight, coordination, and support for multiple programs and their interdependencies

Explanation: A Program Portfolio Management Office (PPMO) provides centralized oversight, coordination, and support for multiple programs and their interdependencies within an organization.

450. Question: What is the primary goal of program stakeholder communication?

A) To allocate resources to program activities

B) To track program schedule performance

C) To provide relevant and timely information to program stakeholders

D) To manage program finances

Answer: C) To provide relevant and timely information to program stakeholders

Explanation: The primary goal of program stakeholder communication is to provide relevant and timely information to program stakeholders, ensuring they are well-informed and engaged in program activities.

451. Question: What is the primary purpose of a Program Benefit Realization Plan?

A) To allocate resources to program activities

B) To track program schedule performance

C) To outline how program benefits will be identified, measured, and realized

D) To create a detailed program budget

Answer: C) To outline how program benefits will be identified, measured, and realized

Explanation: A Program Benefit Realization Plan outlines how program benefits will be identified, measured, and realized, ensuring that program objectives are met.

452. Question: In program management, what does the term "Program Dependency Analysis" refer to?

A) A tool for tracking program finances

B) A process for identifying and managing program dependencies

C) A method for documenting program risks

D) A technique for estimating program durations

Answer: B) A process for identifying and managing program dependencies

Explanation: Program Dependency Analysis involves the process of identifying and managing program dependencies to ensure coordination and successful execution.

453. Question: What is the primary purpose of a Program Stakeholder Communication Plan?

A) To allocate resources to program activities

B) To track program schedule performance

C) To outline how program communication with stakeholders will be planned and executed

D) To create a detailed program budget

Answer: C) To outline how program communication with stakeholders will be planned and executed

Explanation: A Program Stakeholder Communication Plan outlines how program communication with stakeholders will be planned and executed, ensuring effective engagement.

454. Question: What is the primary focus of program resource allocation?

A) To assess program risks

B) To allocate resources to program activities optimally

C) To manage program finances

D) To ensure program compliance with regulations

Answer: B) To allocate resources to program activities optimally

Explanation: The primary focus of program resource allocation is to allocate resources to program activities optimally, ensuring efficient resource utilization.

455. Question: In program management, what does the term "Program Dependency Mapping" refer to?

A) A tool for tracking program finances

B) A process for identifying and managing program dependencies

C) A method for documenting program risks

D) A technique for estimating program durations

Answer: B) A process for identifying and managing program dependencies

Explanation: Program Dependency Mapping involves the process of identifying and managing program dependencies to ensure coordination and successful execution.

456. Question: What is the primary purpose of a Program Benefits Dependency Matrix?

A) To allocate resources to program activities

B) To track program schedule performance

C) To document and analyze the dependencies between program benefits

D) To create a detailed program budget

Answer: C) To document and analyze the dependencies between program benefits

Explanation: A Program Benefits Dependency Matrix is used to document and analyze the dependencies between program benefits, ensuring a clear understanding of how they relate to each other.

457. Question: In program management, what does the term "Program Benefits Realization" refer to?

A) The allocation of resources to program activities

B) The measurement of program schedule performance

C) The process of identifying, tracking, and realizing program benefits

D) The creation of a detailed program budget

Answer: C) The process of identifying, tracking, and realizing program benefits

Explanation: Program Benefits Realization refers to the process of identifying, tracking, and realizing program benefits to achieve program objectives.

458. Question: What is the primary purpose of a Program Governance Charter?

A) To allocate resources to program activities

B) To track program schedule performance

C) To define the program's governance framework, authority, and responsibilities

D) To create a detailed program budget

Answer: C) To define the program's governance framework, authority, and responsibilities

Explanation: A Program Governance Charter is used to define the program's governance framework, authority, and responsibilities, ensuring clear governance guidelines.

459. Question: What is the primary focus of program stakeholder engagement?

A) To allocate resources to program activities

B) To assess program benefits realization

C) To build positive relationships and foster collaboration with program stakeholders

D) To create a detailed program budget

Answer: C) To build positive relationships and foster collaboration with program stakeholders

Explanation: The primary focus of program stakeholder engagement is to build positive relationships and foster collaboration with program stakeholders, promoting their active involvement in the program.

460. Question: What is the primary purpose of a Program Benefits Dependency Matrix?

A) To allocate resources to program activities

B) To track program schedule performance

C) To document and analyze the dependencies between program benefits

D) To create a detailed program budget

Answer: C) To document and analyze the dependencies between program benefits

Explanation: A Program Benefits Dependency Matrix is used to document and analyze the dependencies between program benefits, ensuring a clear understanding of how they relate to each other.

461. Question: What is the primary purpose of a Program Governance Framework?

A) To allocate resources to program activities

B) To define the program's scope and objectives

C) To establish the structure, roles, and responsibilities for program governance

D) To create a detailed program schedule

Answer: C) To establish the structure, roles, and responsibilities for program governance

Explanation: A Program Governance Framework is used to establish the structure, roles, and responsibilities for program governance, ensuring effective oversight.

462. Question: What is the primary goal of program quality management?

A) To allocate resources to program activities

B) To assess program benefits realization

C) To ensure that program processes and deliverables meet established quality standards

D) To create a detailed program budget

Answer: C) To ensure that program processes and deliverables meet established quality standards

Explanation: The primary goal of program quality management is to ensure that program processes and deliverables meet established quality standards, promoting quality throughout the program.

463. Question: What is the primary purpose of a Program Risk Mitigation Plan?

A) To allocate resources to program activities

B) To document and track program risks and their potential impact

C) To assess program financial performance

D) To create a detailed program schedule

Answer: B) To document and track program risks and their potential impact

Explanation: A Program Risk Mitigation Plan is used to document and track program risks and their potential impact on the program's objectives.

464. Question: Which program management role is responsible for providing funding, resources, and strategic alignment to the program?

A) Program Manager

B) Program Sponsor

C) Program Coordinator

D) Program Governance Board

Answer: B) Program Sponsor

Explanation: The Program Sponsor is responsible for providing funding, resources, and strategic alignment to the program.

465. Question: What is the primary focus of program resource allocation?

A) To assess program risks

B) To allocate resources to program activities optimally

C) To manage program finances

D) To ensure program compliance with regulations

Answer: B) To allocate resources to program activities optimally

Explanation: The primary focus of program resource allocation is to allocate resources to program activities optimally, ensuring efficient resource utilization.

466. Question: In program management, what does the term "Program Dependency Analysis" refer to?

A) A tool for tracking program finances

B) A process for identifying and managing program dependencies

C) A method for documenting program risks

D) A technique for estimating program durations

Answer: B) A process for identifying and managing program dependencies

Explanation: Program Dependency Analysis involves the process of identifying and managing program dependencies to ensure coordination and successful execution.

467. Question: What is the primary purpose of a Program Communication Plan?

A) To allocate resources to program activities

B) To track program schedule performance

C) To outline how program communication will be managed and executed

D) To create a detailed program budget

Answer: C) To outline how program communication will be managed and executed

Explanation: A Program Communication Plan outlines how program communication will be managed and executed, ensuring effective stakeholder communication.

468. Question: What is the primary goal of program stakeholder engagement?

A) To allocate resources to program activities

B) To assess program benefits realization

C) To build positive relationships and foster collaboration with program stakeholders

D) To create a detailed program budget

Answer: C) To build positive relationships and foster collaboration with program stakeholders

Explanation: The primary goal of program stakeholder engagement is to build positive relationships and foster collaboration with program stakeholders, promoting their active involvement in the program.

469. Question: What is the primary purpose of a Program Portfolio Management Office (PPMO)?

A) To allocate resources to program activities

B) To track program schedule performance

C) To provide centralized oversight, coordination, and support for multiple programs and their interdependencies

D) To create a detailed program budget

Answer: C) To provide centralized oversight, coordination, and support for multiple programs and their interdependencies

Explanation: A Program Portfolio Management Office (PPMO) provides centralized oversight, coordination, and support for multiple programs and their interdependencies within an organization.

470. Question: What is the primary goal of program stakeholder communication?

A) To allocate resources to program activities

B) To track program schedule performance

C) To provide relevant and timely information to program stakeholders

D) To manage program finances

Answer: C) To provide relevant and timely information to program stakeholders

Explanation: The primary goal of program stakeholder communication is to provide relevant and timely information to program stakeholders, ensuring they are well-informed and engaged in program activities.

471. Question: What is the primary purpose of a Program Benefit Realization Plan?

A) To allocate resources to program activities

B) To track program schedule performance

C) To outline how program benefits will be identified, measured, and realized

D) To create a detailed program budget

Answer: C) To outline how program benefits will be identified, measured, and realized

Explanation: A Program Benefit Realization Plan outlines how program benefits will be identified, measured, and realized, ensuring that program objectives are met.

472. Question: In program management, what does the term "Program Dependency Analysis" refer to?

A) A tool for tracking program finances

B) A process for identifying and managing program dependencies

C) A method for documenting program risks

D) A technique for estimating program durations

Answer: B) A process for identifying and managing program dependencies

Explanation: Program Dependency Analysis involves the process of identifying and managing program dependencies to ensure coordination and successful execution.

473. Question: What is the primary purpose of a Program Stakeholder Communication Plan?

A) To allocate resources to program activities

B) To track program schedule performance

C) To outline how program communication with stakeholders will be planned and executed

D) To create a detailed program budget

Answer: C) To outline how program communication with stakeholders will be planned and executed

Explanation: A Program Stakeholder Communication Plan outlines how program communication with stakeholders will be planned and executed, ensuring effective engagement.

474. Question: What is the primary focus of program risk management?

A) To allocate resources to program activities

B) To track program schedule performance

C) To identify, assess, and mitigate program risks

D) To create a detailed program budget

Answer: C) To identify, assess, and mitigate program risks

Explanation: The primary focus of program risk management is to identify, assess, and mitigate program risks to minimize their potential impact on the program.

475. Question: In program management, what does the term "Program Benefits Dependency Matrix" refer to?

A) A tool for tracking program finances

B) A process for identifying and managing program dependencies

C) A method for documenting program risks

D) A technique for estimating program durations

Answer: B) A process for identifying and managing program dependencies

Explanation: Program Benefits Dependency Matrix refers to the process of identifying and managing program dependencies to ensure successful program execution.

476. Question: What is the primary purpose of a Program Risk Register?

A) To allocate resources to program activities

B) To track program schedule performance

C) To document and manage program risks and their potential impact

D) To create a detailed program budget

Answer: C) To document and manage program risks and their potential impact

Explanation: A Program Risk Register is used to document and manage program risks and their potential impact on the program's objectives.

477. Question: What is the primary purpose of a Program Stakeholder Engagement Plan?

A) To allocate resources to program activities

B) To track program schedule performance

C) To outline how program stakeholders will be engaged and their needs addressed

D) To create a detailed program budget

Answer: C) To outline how program stakeholders will be engaged and their needs addressed

Explanation: A Program Stakeholder Engagement Plan outlines how program stakeholders will be engaged and their needs addressed to ensure their active involvement.

478. Question: In program management, what does the term "Program Benefits Realization" refer to?

A) The allocation of resources to program activities

B) The measurement of program schedule performance

C) The process of identifying, tracking, and realizing program benefits

D) The creation of a detailed program budget

Answer: C) The process of identifying, tracking, and realizing program benefits

Explanation: Program Benefits Realization refers to the process of identifying, tracking, and realizing program benefits to achieve program objectives.

479. Question: What is the primary purpose of a Program Governance Charter?

A) To allocate resources to program activities

B) To track program schedule performance

C) To define the program's governance framework, authority, and responsibilities

D) To create a detailed program budget

Answer: C) To define the program's governance framework, authority, and responsibilities

Explanation: A Program Governance Charter is used to define the program's governance framework, authority, and responsibilities, ensuring clear governance guidelines.

480. Question: What is the primary focus of program stakeholder engagement?

A) To allocate resources to program activities

B) To assess program benefits realization

C) To build positive relationships and foster collaboration with program stakeholders

D) To create a detailed program budget

Answer: C) To build positive relationships and foster collaboration with program stakeholders

Explanation: The primary focus of program stakeholder engagement is to build positive relationships and foster collaboration with program stakeholders, promoting their active involvement in the program.

481. Question: What is the primary purpose of a Program Governance Framework?

A) To allocate resources to program activities

B) To define the program's scope and objectives

C) To establish the structure, roles, and responsibilities for program governance

D) To create a detailed program schedule

Answer: C) To establish the structure, roles, and responsibilities for program governance

Explanation: A Program Governance Framework is used to establish the structure, roles, and responsibilities for program governance, ensuring effective oversight.

482. Question: What is the primary goal of program quality management?

A) To allocate resources to program activities

B) To assess program benefits realization

C) To ensure that program processes and deliverables meet established quality standards

D) To create a detailed program budget

Answer: C) To ensure that program processes and deliverables meet established quality standards

Explanation: The primary goal of program quality management is to ensure that program processes and deliverables meet established quality standards, promoting quality throughout the program.

483. Question: What is the primary purpose of a Program Risk Mitigation Plan?

A) To allocate resources to program activities

B) To document and track program risks and their potential impact

C) To assess program financial performance

D) To create a detailed program schedule

Answer: B) To document and track program risks and their potential impact

Explanation: A Program Risk Mitigation Plan is used to document and track program risks and their potential impact on the program's objectives.

484. Question: Which program management role is responsible for providing funding, resources, and strategic alignment to the program?

A) Program Manager

B) Program Sponsor

C) Program Coordinator

D) Program Governance Board

Answer: B) Program Sponsor

Explanation: The Program Sponsor is responsible for providing funding, resources, and strategic alignment to the program.

485. Question: What is the primary focus of program resource allocation?

A) To assess program risks

B) To allocate resources to program activities optimally

C) To manage program finances

D) To ensure program compliance with regulations

Answer: B) To allocate resources to program activities optimally

Explanation: The primary focus of program resource allocation is to allocate resources to program activities optimally, ensuring efficient resource utilization.

486. Question: In program management, what does the term "Program Dependency Analysis" refer to?

A) A tool for tracking program finances

B) A process for identifying and managing program dependencies

C) A method for documenting program risks

D) A technique for estimating program durations

Answer: B) A process for identifying and managing program dependencies

Explanation: Program Dependency Analysis involves the process of identifying and managing program dependencies to ensure coordination and successful execution.

487. Question: What is the primary purpose of a Program Communication Plan?

A) To allocate resources to program activities

B) To track program schedule performance

C) To outline how program communication will be managed and executed

D) To create a detailed program budget

Answer: C) To outline how program communication will be managed and executed

Explanation: A Program Communication Plan outlines how program communication will be managed and executed, ensuring effective stakeholder communication.

488. Question: What is the primary goal of program stakeholder engagement?

A) To allocate resources to program activities

B) To assess program benefits realization

C) To build positive relationships and foster collaboration with program stakeholders

D) To create a detailed program budget

Answer: C) To build positive relationships and foster collaboration with program stakeholders

Explanation: The primary goal of program stakeholder engagement is to build positive relationships and foster collaboration with program stakeholders, promoting their active involvement in the program.

489. Question: What is the primary purpose of a Program Portfolio Management Office (PPMO)?

A) To allocate resources to program activities

B) To track program schedule performance

C) To provide centralized oversight, coordination, and support for multiple programs and their interdependencies

D) To create a detailed program budget

Answer: C) To provide centralized oversight, coordination, and support for multiple programs and their interdependencies

Explanation: A Program Portfolio Management Office (PPMO) provides centralized oversight, coordination, and support for multiple programs and their interdependencies within an organization.

490. Question: What is the primary goal of program stakeholder communication?

A) To allocate resources to program activities

B) To track program schedule performance

C) To provide relevant and timely information to program stakeholders

D) To manage program finances

Answer: C) To provide relevant and timely information to program stakeholders

Explanation: The primary goal of program stakeholder communication is to provide relevant and timely information to program stakeholders, ensuring they are well-informed and engaged in program activities.

491. Question: What is the primary purpose of a Program Benefit Realization Plan?

A) To allocate resources to program activities

B) To track program schedule performance

C) To outline how program benefits will be identified, measured, and realized

D) To create a detailed program budget

Answer: C) To outline how program benefits will be identified, measured, and realized

Explanation: A Program Benefit Realization Plan outlines how program benefits will be identified, measured, and realized, ensuring that program objectives are met.

492. Question: In program management, what does the term "Program Dependency Analysis" refer to?

A) A tool for tracking program finances

B) A process for identifying and managing program dependencies

C) A method for documenting program risks

D) A technique for estimating program durations

Answer: B) A process for identifying and managing program dependencies

Explanation: Program Dependency Analysis involves the process of identifying and managing program dependencies to ensure coordination and successful execution.

493. Question: What is the primary purpose of a Program Stakeholder Communication Plan?

A) To allocate resources to program activities

B) To track program schedule performance

C) To outline how program communication with stakeholders will be planned and executed

D) To create a detailed program budget

Answer: C) To outline how program communication with stakeholders will be planned and executed

Explanation: A Program Stakeholder Communication Plan outlines how program communication with stakeholders will be planned and executed, ensuring effective engagement.

494. Question: What is the primary focus of program risk management?

A) To allocate resources to program activities

B) To track program schedule performance

C) To identify, assess, and mitigate program risks

D) To create a detailed program budget

Answer: C) To identify, assess, and mitigate program risks

Explanation: The primary focus of program risk management is to identify, assess, and mitigate program risks to minimize their potential impact on the program.

495. Question: In program management, what does the term "Program Benefits Dependency Matrix" refer to?

A) A tool for tracking program finances

B) A process for identifying and managing program dependencies

C) A method for documenting program risks

D) A technique for estimating program durations

Answer: B) A process for identifying and managing program dependencies

Explanation: Program Benefits Dependency Matrix refers to the process of identifying and managing program dependencies to ensure successful program execution.

496. Question: What is the primary purpose of a Program Risk Register?

A) To allocate resources to program activities

B) To track program schedule performance

C) To document and manage program risks and their potential impact

D) To create a detailed program budget

Answer: C) To document and manage program risks and their potential impact

Explanation: A Program Risk Register is used to document and manage program risks and their potential impact on the program's objectives.

497. Question: What is the primary purpose of a Program Stakeholder Engagement Plan?

A) To allocate resources to program activities

B) To track program schedule performance

C) To outline how program stakeholders will be engaged and their needs addressed

D) To create a detailed program budget

Answer: C) To outline how program stakeholders will be engaged and their needs addressed

Explanation: A Program Stakeholder Engagement Plan outlines how program stakeholders will be engaged and their needs addressed to ensure their active involvement.

498. Question: In program management, what does the term "Program Benefits Realization" refer to?

A) The allocation of resources to program activities

B) The measurement of program schedule performance

C) The process of identifying, tracking, and realizing program benefits

D) The creation of a detailed program budget

Answer: C) The process of identifying, tracking, and realizing program benefits

Explanation: Program Benefits Realization refers to the process of identifying, tracking, and realizing program benefits to achieve program objectives.

499. Question: What is the primary purpose of a Program Governance Charter?

A) To allocate resources to program activities

B) To track program schedule performance

C) To define the program's governance framework, authority, and responsibilities

D) To create a detailed program budget

Answer: C) To define the program's governance framework, authority, and responsibilities

Explanation: A Program Governance Charter is used to define the program's governance framework, authority, and responsibilities, ensuring clear governance guidelines.

500. Question: What is the primary focus of program stakeholder engagement?

A) To allocate resources to program activities

B) To assess program benefits realization

C) To build positive relationships and foster collaboration with program stakeholders

D) To create a detailed program budget

Answer: C) To build positive relationships and foster collaboration with program stakeholders

Explanation: The primary focus of program stakeholder engagement is to build positive relationships and foster collaboration with program stakeholders, promoting their active involvement in the program.

501. Question: In program management, what is the primary purpose of a Program Benefit Realization Plan?

A) To allocate resources to program activities

B) To define the program's scope and objectives

C) To outline how program benefits will be identified, measured, and realized

D) To create a detailed program schedule

Answer: C) To outline how program benefits will be identified, measured, and realized

Explanation: A Program Benefit Realization Plan outlines how program benefits will be identified, measured, and realized, ensuring that program objectives are met.

502. Question: What is the primary goal of program risk management?

A) To allocate resources to program activities

B) To track program schedule performance

C) To identify, assess, and mitigate program risks

D) To create a detailed program budget

Answer: C) To identify, assess, and mitigate program risks

Explanation: The primary goal of program risk management is to identify, assess, and mitigate program risks to minimize their potential impact on the program.

503. Question: What is the primary purpose of a Program Governance Charter?

A) To allocate resources to program activities

B) To track program schedule performance

C) To define the program's governance framework, authority, and responsibilities

D) To create a detailed program budget

Answer: C) To define the program's governance framework, authority, and responsibilities

Explanation: A Program Governance Charter is used to define the program's governance framework, authority, and responsibilities, ensuring clear governance guidelines.

504. Question: In program management, what does the term "Program Benefits Dependency Matrix" refer to?

A) A tool for tracking program finances

B) A process for identifying and managing program dependencies

C) A method for documenting program risks

D) A technique for estimating program durations

Answer: B) A process for identifying and managing program dependencies

Explanation: Program Benefits Dependency Matrix refers to the process of identifying and managing program dependencies to ensure successful program execution.

505. Question: What is the primary focus of program resource allocation?

A) To assess program risks

B) To allocate resources to program activities optimally

C) To manage program finances

D) To ensure program compliance with regulations

Answer: B) To allocate resources to program activities optimally

Explanation: The primary focus of program resource allocation is to allocate resources to program activities optimally, ensuring efficient resource utilization.

506. Question: What is the primary purpose of a Program Risk Register?

A) To allocate resources to program activities

B) To track program schedule performance

C) To document and manage program risks and their potential impact

D) To create a detailed program budget

Answer: C) To document and manage program risks and their potential impact

Explanation: A Program Risk Register is used to document and manage program risks and their potential impact on the program's objectives.

507. Question: What is the primary goal of program stakeholder communication?

A) To allocate resources to program activities

B) To track program schedule performance

C) To provide relevant and timely information to program stakeholders

D) To manage program finances

Answer: C) To provide relevant and timely information to program stakeholders

Explanation: The primary goal of program stakeholder communication is to provide relevant and timely information to program stakeholders, ensuring they are well-informed and engaged in program activities.

508. Question: What is the primary focus of program governance?

A) To allocate resources to program activities

B) To define the program's scope and objectives

C) To establish the structure, roles, and responsibilities for program governance

D) To create a detailed program schedule

Answer: C) To establish the structure, roles, and responsibilities for program governance

Explanation: The primary focus of program governance is to establish the structure, roles, and responsibilities for program governance, ensuring effective oversight.

509. Question: What role is responsible for providing funding, resources, and strategic alignment to a program?

A) Program Manager

B) Program Coordinator

C) Program Sponsor

D) Program Stakeholder

Answer: C) Program Sponsor

Explanation: The Program Sponsor is responsible for providing funding, resources, and strategic alignment to the program.

510. Question: What is the primary goal of program stakeholder engagement?

A) To allocate resources to program activities

B) To assess program benefits realization

C) To build positive relationships and foster collaboration with program stakeholders

D) To create a detailed program budget

Answer: C) To build positive relationships and foster collaboration with program stakeholders

Explanation: The primary goal of program stakeholder engagement is to build positive relationships and foster collaboration with program stakeholders, promoting their active involvement in the program.

END NOTE

As you conclude your journey through "PMI-PgMP Exam Excellence: Q&A with In-Depth Explanations," we hope you're leaving with a heightened understanding of program management and a strong foundation for achieving your Program Management Professional (PgMP) certification.

Obtaining PgMP certification is more than a badge of honour; it's a testament to your dedication, expertise, and commitment to excellence in program management. With this certification, you're not just advancing your career; you're contributing to the growth and success of your organization.

Remember that certification is a milestone, not the destination. Your expertise in program management will continue to evolve and provide value to your projects and programs. Keep refining your skills, stay updated with industry trends, and foster a mindset of continuous improvement.

As you prepare to embark on your PgMP exam, maintain a confident and focused approach. Take advantage of the knowledge gained from this book, leverage practical insights, and practice diligently. You've demonstrated the dedication to reach this point, and success in the exam is well within your grasp.

We extend our best wishes as you step forward to attain your PgMP certification and further elevate your career in program management. Your commitment to excellence will undoubtedly make a lasting impact on the projects and programs you lead.

Best of luck on your journey to becoming a certified Program Management Professional!

**Please note that the example questions provided are for illustrative purposes only and may not reflect the actual questions found in the PMI-PgMP exam. The purpose is to give you an idea of the question format and provide practice in applying your knowledge. It's important to refer to the official PMI resources and study materials to prepare thoroughly for the exam.

• • • •

**WE APOLOGIZE FOR ANY inadvertent repetition of questions in this material. Please rest assured that any instances of repeated questions were not intentional. If you come across any such occurrences, kindly excuse us, and we appreciate your understanding. Our aim is to provide you with comprehensive and unique content to enhance your learning experience and we're here to support you.

Also by SUJAN

PMP Practice Test Navigator: Nailing the Exam
PMP Success: Ultimate Exam Questions & Answers
PMP Exam Companion
CAPM Success Blueprint
AgileQuest: Unlocking PMI-ACP Success
PMI-RMP Exam Companion
PMI-PBA Exam Success :A Practical Guide to Ace Business Analysis
Questions
CAPM Success Path : MCQs and Explanations for Prep Excellence
CAPM Q-Connect
CAPM Exam Insights: Q&A with Explanations
PMI-ACP Success Path: Q&A with Explanations
PMI-ACP Exam Insights: Q&A with Explanations
PMI-PgMP Exam Insights: Q&A with Explanations
PMI-SP Success Blueprint: Q&A with Explanations
PMI-RMP Success Blueprint :Q&A with Explanations
PfMP Exam Companion: Q&A with Explanations
PMP Exam Insights: Q&A with Explanations
PMI-RMP Exam Insights: Q&A with Explanations
PMI-PgMP Exam Companion: Q&A with Explanations
CAPM Essentials: Expert Q&A with Detailed Explanations
PMI-PgMP Exam Excellence: Q&A with In-Depth Explanations

Milton Keynes UK
Ingram Content Group UK Ltd.
UKHW020829191223
434651UK00015B/808